D0709950

ci

Emery Vincent Design

Brochures3

An International Compilation of Brochure Design
Broschürendesign im internationalen Überblick
Une compilation internationale sur le design des brochures

Publisher and Creative Director: B. Martin Pedersen

Editor: Heinke Jenssen
Assistant Editors: April Heck, Vivian Babuts, Laura Cramer

Art Director: Massimo Acanfora
Graphic Designers: Delfin Chavez, Carol Ford
Photographer: Alfredo Parraga

Published by Graphis Inc.

(opposite) Emery Vincent Design *(following page)* The Attik *(page 6)* Crosby Associates Inc.

Contents Inhalt Sommaire

marks: We extend our heartfelt thanks to contributors ~~th~~oughout the world who have made it possible to publish ~~w~~ide and international spectrum of the best work in the ~~fiel~~d of brochure design Entry instructions for all Graphis ~~Bo~~oks may be requested from: **Graphis Inc.**, 141 Lexing-~~ton~~ Avenue, New York, NY 10016-8193 or visit our Web ~~site~~, www.graphis.com

Anmerkungen: Unser Dank gilt den Einsendern aus aller Welt, die es uns durch ihre Beiträge ermöglicht haben, ein breites, internationales Specktrum der besten Arbeiten zu veröffentlichen. Teilnahmebedingungen für die Graphis-Bücher sind erhältlich bei: **Graphis Inc.**, 141 Lexington Avenue, New York, NY 10016-8193. Besuchen Sie uns im World Wide Web, www.graphis.com

Remerciements: Nous remercions les participants du monde entier qui ont rendu possible la publication de cet ouvrage offrant un panorama complet des meilleurs travaux. Les modalités d'inscription peuvent être obtenues auprès de: **Graphis Inc.**, 141 Lexington Avenue, New York, NY 10016-8193. Rendez-nous visite sur notre site web: www.graphis.com

Designframe: An Interview by Sarah Haun

Reflecting on their long-time relationships with Martex and Strathmore Papers, Designframe

principals James Sebastian and Michael McGinn talk about brochures: what distinguishes

the best from the others, the creative process, and why an educated team can sometimes make

all the difference. Sebastian founded Designframe, a graphic design firm in New York City,

in 1976. McGinn worked as a senior designer with Designframe in the 1980s—during the

production of its celebrated brochure series for Martex home textiles—and re-joined the firm

as a partner in 1994. In addition to serving clients in a variety of businesses, Designframe

are currently design consultants to Strathmore, a fine papers division of International Paper

Corporation, collaborating with the company in marketing and product development, and

working as always to take brochure design above and beyond the places it's been before.

Sarah Haun is a communications consultant who lives in Brooklyn, New York. She works with graphic designers, architects and industrial designers and enjoys writing about the creative process for print and interactive media. Her work has appeared in publications including ABITARE, HOW, STEP-BY-STEP, GRAPHIS and IDEA. (pictured opposite) Designframe was responsible for creating brochures for Martex home textiles from 1980-1994. An unusually open-ended design process included explorations of form, materials, and bindings that strengthened the object value of the pieces. (Project photography by Bruce Wolf and Joe Standart.)

Sarah Haun: What's your idea of a brochure?

James Sebastian: A printed piece that's larger than a flyer and smaller than a book. That's pretty open-ended, pretty exciting as a design problem.

Michael McGinn: Sometimes there is some formal element—shape, binding method, material—that can give the brochure value as an object. An aluminum cover, a leather cover with beautifully rounded corners, some nice debossing: these things are seductive to begin with. It's one of the reasons the Martex pieces worked so well.

SH: Fifteen years ago, your work for Martex introduced a new approach to the form: wordless, fantasy-oriented stories built from beautiful photographs and flawless production. How did it happen?

JS: It started with a fairly sophisticated client who'd already had a history of working with terrific designers. We also put together an extraordinary team—photographers, stylist, printers—and were able to control the process all the way through. We weren't just taking a picture of a room, we were trying to create an emotional feeling. To make it work, we had to be totally involved in developing the concept, the form, the art direction, the mechanics of printing. It was like making a movie: the designer was the producer and the director, having that one vision to hold the project together, orchestrating it from beginning to end. But it wasn't planned every step of the way, there was a lot of experimentation.

SH: You did over thirty brochures over the course of the relationship. Where did you keep finding inspiration?

JS: The inspiration came from the various members of the team, a very strong, educated team. Sometimes it came from Martex's product design, or a photographic approach, or a format. We always started off with some open-ended direction and then set our own constraints. The decisions took place with the team working together on the spot. We didn't have to do a layout and get the client's approval before we could go on to the next step. That's very different. That *is* the difference: earning the client's trust so you can tell them something about what they're going to get but then, in the process, giving them something better.

MM: Designers have to work with the client's real expectations and requirements. It's not about trying to push an idea through.

SH: Why do good ideas sometimes get lost in the execution?

JS: Sometimes too many parameters get locked in too early. They become so confining that you don't have that ability to take advantage of spontaneity, of recognizing something that you didn't think of initially. That's such an important part of the creative process. The down side is that once you have all this responsibility, you better not mess up! But if you continue to do your job right, you might get to do thirty projects, one after another.

MM: The Martex brochures were conventional in their linear, story-telling construction, but otherwise, they broke a lot of conventions. They were beautiful books—great color printing, great production standards—more than anybody had ever seen before. Designers took notice. It was educational stuff. There aren't that many conventions to be broken anymore. There's still a place for outrage, but in the long run, content matters a great deal. Appropriateness matters. Effectiveness matters. The Martex work was a marriage of appropriateness and effectiveness and execution. Given the point in time, it was an eye-opener.

JS: There are always a few companies that stand out because they are interested in the quality of ideas, in working with the be designers, the best writers. Talent. It goes back as far as Strathmo working with the innovative designer, printmaker, and illustrat Will Bradley at the turn of the century. There was Bradbu Thompson's pioneering and educational work for Westvac Inspirations in the '40s and '50s. There was John Massey's "Gre Ideas of Western Man" campaign for Container Corporation the 1960s and '70s. There was the "Imagination" series Jim Mih did for Champion in the '70s and '80s. They stood out. The pap companies started a tradition of hiring designers to push the sta of the art of design and production. It's exciting for us to b involved in that with Strathmore now; they've continued th tradition. They really give a gift to the graphic arts industry and w all benefit from that.

MM: With Strathmore the work process is not quite as organi but there's still something left to chance. There's more planning u front in terms of what a brochure needs to accomplish, how it going to work with other pieces to communicate the qualities the paper products, the quality of the company. Togethe materials, visuals, text and form have to speak in a single, consister voice, to communicate one fairly solid message.

SH: Why is the object quality of a brochure so important?

MM: There's the way the paper prints and performs, the play the surfaces against one another. When there's a perfect marriag of the message and the materials, a brochure invites a differen kind of response. I'm not sure the recipient knows what they' appreciating on a conscious level, but I do think most people hav an innate appreciation for quality.

JS: If you respond to an appealing object, even though you ma not be the intended audience, you can be sure that the intende audience will feel something, too. I think that's where successf brochures transcend their basic purpose: in the interaction of th imagery, the texture and weight of the paper, what it feels like i your hands. A designer can be in control of these tactile qualitie and what they communicate.

SH: Then what's the point of a book about brochures, if you can handle the object?

MM: You lose some of the material qualities and scale that are a important part of the message, but you can still develop a appreciation for certain ideas and certain effects.

JS: This is a book designed by designers for designers. Potentia clients look at these, too, but generally they're looking for wha they think is the solution to their own problem.

MM: For clients it's not about the process, it's about the solution A client needs a brochure to serve some specific purpose, to move a product or to get an idea across to a group of people. There are specific objectives, budgets, and schedules that have to be balance against the need to attract some attention to the idea. Done well brochures are a pretty wonderful little experience. I keep brochure occasionally, whether I want the product that's in it o not, because it was well done.

JS: It feels too good to throw away. You may never refer to i again, but you *think* you will, so you keep it.

MM: I have respect for other designers' work for that reason. We all wrestle with similar problems and similar constraints. We look at books like these to see how others have broken through and solved them in new ways. It's fun. We also look to see which clients have learned how to benefit from the creative process. The educated clients. The kind of clients we enjoy working with.

THE STRATHMORE TEXTURE GROUP

AMERICANA BEAU BRILLIANT FIESTA   GRANDEE PASTELLE RHODODENDRON

STRATHMORE TEXT & COVER

THE STRATHMORE TEXTURE GROUP

AMERICANA BEAU BRILLIANT FIESTA GRANDEE PASTELLE RHODODENDRON

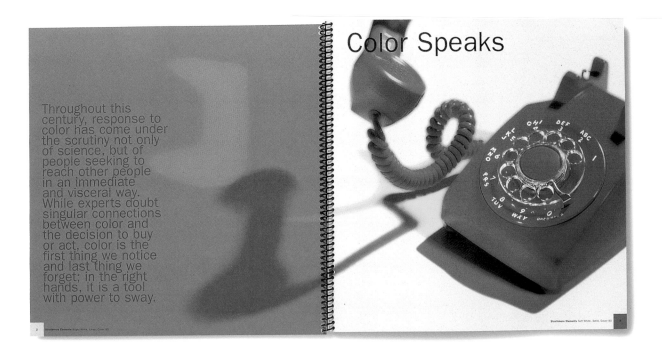

Color Speaks

Throughout this century, response to color has come under the scrutiny not only of science, but of people seeking to reach other people in an immediate and visceral way. While experts doubt singular connections between color and the decision to buy or act, color is the first thing we notice and last thing we forget; in the right hands, it is a tool with power to sway.

(previous page)
Brochures like this mega-swatch-book for Strathmore transcend their basic purpose through the interaction of the imagery, texture, weight of paper, and the structure of the presentation. "The designer is control of these tactile qualities and what they communicate," says Sebastian.

(this spread)
The "Psychology of Color" series for Strathmore explored human response to color and how these perceptions and associations have been used in the marketplace. (Photography by David Arky.)

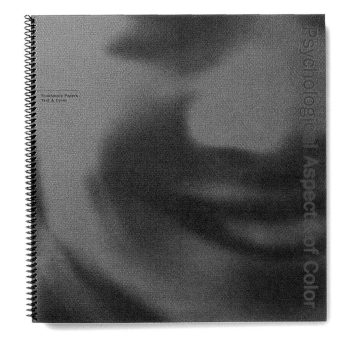

Color Motivates

By the 1920s, color was a science, its impact studied, its application carefully calculated to attract, seduce, comfort and sway. "In the 40s and 50s, the use of color was pioneering," says color consultant Davis Masten. "But today there's not a single category out there that doesn't use color in the marketing arsenal."

Who wears what

marketable aspects of color

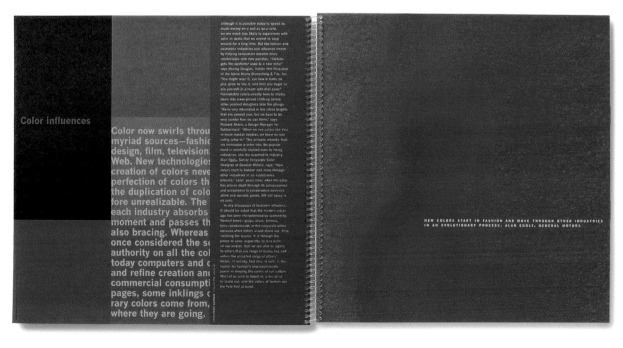

Color influences

Color now swirls throu
myriad sources—fashio
design, film, television
Web. New technologies
creation of colors neve
perfection of colors th
the duplication of colo
fore unrealizable. The
each industry absorbs
moment and passes th
also bracing. Whereas
once considered the so
authority on all the col
today computers and c
and refine creation and
commercial consumpti
pages, some inklings o
rary colors come from,
where they are going.

NEW COLORS START IN FASHION AND MOVE THROUGH OTHER INDUSTRIES
IN AN EVOLUTIONARY PROCESS. ALAN EGGLY, GENERAL MOTORS

ZIMBABWE

UNTIL RECENTLY, THREE COLORS, WHITE, RED and black, have predominated across the continent of Africa. These most primal of all colors were readily available: white from kaolin or lime, red from ocher or kola nuts, and black from mud or charcoal. ✦ It is a fact that in all languages these are also the first three colors to be named. Inevitably, they also carry the most meaning and are believed to work the greatest magic. White and black represent respectively heaven and earth, the spiritual and the material, feminine and masculine qualities; red is intermediary – a symbol of life and energy (blood and fire). Judicious use of these colors would define a face painter or house decorator's position in society just as clearly as a well-cut, dark business suit in Western culture . . . and could also ward off malevolent spirits. ✦ While age-old color

The "Cultural Aspects of Color" series for Strathmore looks at regional uses and sources of pigments and palettes. The Zimbabwe spread (top) depicts boldly decorated artifacts representing the symbolic power of color in African cultures (Photography by M. Courtney-Clark.) The Japan spread (bottom) celebrates the understanding of the impact of simple color and strong contrasts. (Photography by Neil Selkirk, The Stock Market, Ken Straiton.)

CULTURAL
STRATHMORE
ASPECTS
TEXT & IMAGE
OF COLOR

JAPAN

Brochures 3

34 Wettbewerbsbeiträge

35 Wettbewerbsbeiträge

SPRING
Heizkörper-System

Giovanna Albretti,
Fabrizio Galli
und
Anna Perico,
Berlin

Wasser & Seife
Waschtischarmatur
mit Seifenspender

Thomas Peter,
Gechingen

42 Wettbewerbsbeiträge

Preisverleihung und Preisträger

Bestuhl
Bestuhlungs-System
für Universitäten und
Hörsäle

Christiane Frank
und
Alexander Otto,
Darmstadt

Bow
Türdrücker

André Schelloch,
Stuttgart

26 Wettbewerbsbeiträge

27 Wettbewerbsbeiträge

(opposite)
Design Firm: A. Beinecker
GmbH & Co. KG
Wilke GmbH
Designer: Matthias Holzhauer
Photographer: Gaby Roehle
Client: HEW1 Heinrich Wilke GmbH

(this page)
Design Firm: Werner Schaeppi PR
Art Director: Mark Gilg, Sonya Gilg
Designer: Mark Gilg
Photographer: Claudia Faganini
Copywriter: Werner Schaeppi
Client: BHB–Arhictekten

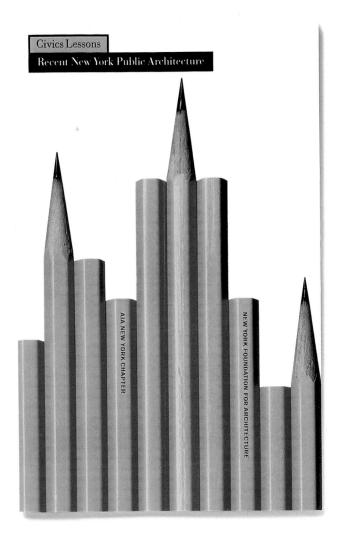

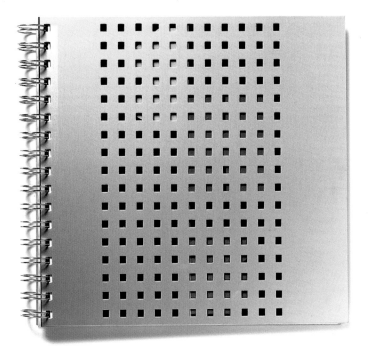

1997 **PREVIA**

TOYOTA

1997 **4RUNNER**

TOYOTA

1997 **COROLLA**

TOYOTA

1997 **TACOMA**

TOYOTA

gency: Saatchi & Saatchi,
s Angeles
eative Director: Dean Van Eimeren
sociate Creative Director:
yle Pastrick
t Directors: Debra Girard,
ren Knecht, David Stokes,
rry Medwig
esigner: Karen Knecht

Photographers: Paul Taylor,
Tim Damon, Rick Graves, Peggy Day,
Rocki Pedersen, Michael Rausch, Joe
Carlson, Todd Johnson
Illustrator: Kevin Hulsey
Copywriters: John Jay, Guinette Wise,
Julie Sandler, Betsy Hamilton
Client: Toyota Motor Sales, USA, Inc.

Design Firm: The Designory, Inc.
Executive Creative Directors: Lannon
Tanchum, Tim Meraz
Creative Director: Carol Funkunaga
Art Directors, Designers: Tim Morra,
Lori Cowherd

Photographers: Rick Rusing, David
LeBon, Joe Carlson, Tim Damon
Copy Creative Director:
Meg Crabtree
Copywriters: John Beck,
Amelia Ostroff
Client: Nissan

Pathfinder SE 4x4 interior shown with optional **Leather Trim Package** in Slate.

mo.

Life is a journey. Enjoy the ride.™

Facts

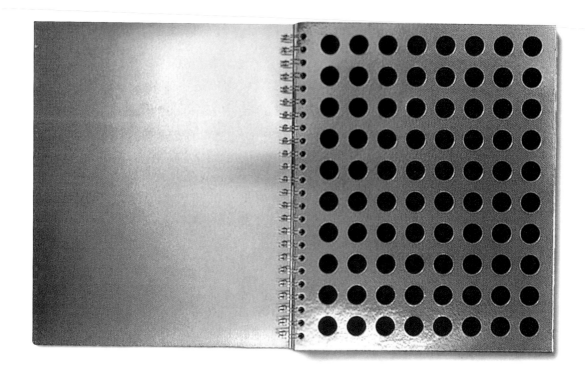

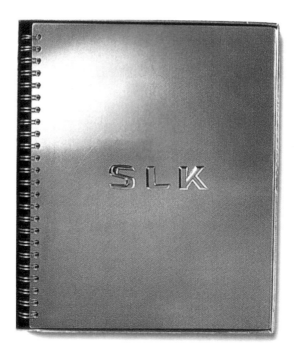

Design Firm: Springer & Jacoby
Creative Directors:
Kurt George Dieckert,
Robert Wohlgemuth, Jan Ritter
Art Directors, Designers: Erik Urmetzer,
Walter Schönauer
Client: Mercedes-Benz AG

(opposite)
Design Firm:
SHR Perceptual Management
Art Directors, Designers:
Dennis Merritt, Karin Burklein Arnold
Photographer: Rodney Rascona
Client: Volkswagen of America

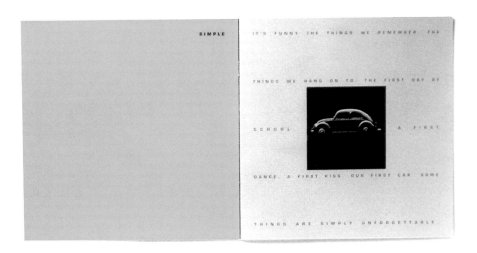

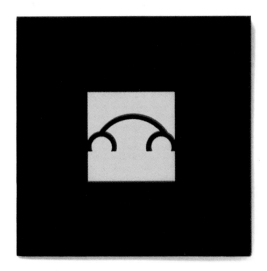

MERCEDES-BENZ
1998 M-CLASS

Specifications and Equipment

Optional sunroof, Package M1 and metallic paint shown.

Optional sunroof, Packages M3 and M4, metallic paint, and dealer-installed accessory road carrier with surfboard attachments shown.

Design Firm: The Designory, Inc.
Art Directors, Designers:
Ulrich Lange, Carolyn Wagner
Photographers: Vic Huber,
Charles Hopkins

Copywriters: Theo Wallace,
Rich Conklin
Client: Mercedes-Benz
of North America

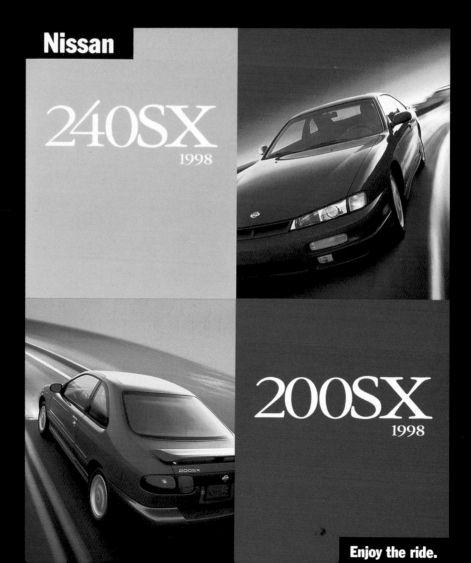

Nissan

240SX
1998

200SX
1998

Enjoy the ride.

Presenting the 1998 Nissan 240SX.

240SX SE shown in **Ultra Red.**

Introducing the New 1998 Nissan 200SX.

YVN 720

200SX SE-R shown in **Deep Crystal Blue.**

Design Firm: The Designory, Inc.
Executive Creative Director:
Lannon Tanchum, Tim Meraz
Creative Director: Carol Fukunaga
Art Director, Designer: Lori Cowherd
Photographers: Rick Rusing,

Peter Lopez,
Tim Damon, Joe Carlson
Copy Creative Director: Meg Crabtree
Copywriter: Gina Lawson
Client: Nissan

Design Firm: Team One Advertising
Creative Director: Tom Cordner
Art Directors: Scott Bremner, Debra Girard
Photographers: Charles Hopkins, Brett Froomer,
Vic Huber, Michael Ruppert
Copywriters: Tom Mescall, Kevin Smith, Eric Walker
Client: Lexus

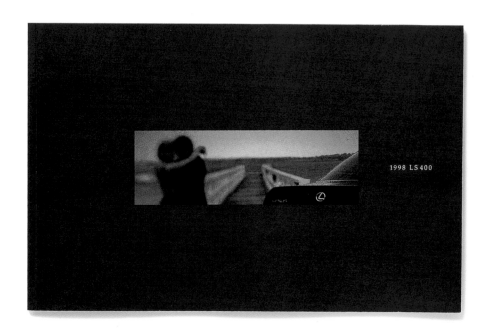

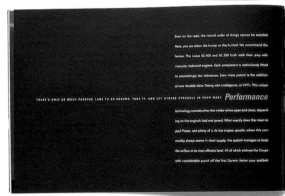

Even on the road, the natural order of things cannot be avoided. Here, you are either the hunter or the hunted. We recommend the former. The Lexus SC 400 and SC 300 both stalk their prey with muscular, balanced engines. Each component is meticulously fitted to astonishingly low tolerances. Even more potent is the addition of new Variable Valve Timing with Intelligence, or VVT-i. This unique THERE'S ONLY SO MUCH PASSING LANE TO GO AROUND. TAKE IT, AND LET OTHERS STRUGGLE IN YOUR WAKE. *Performance* technology controls when the intake valves open and close, depending on the engine's load and speed. What exactly does this mean to you? Power, and plenty of it. At low engine speeds, where this commodity already seems in short supply, the system manages to keep the airflow at its most efficient level. All of which endows the Coupe with considerable punch off the line. Darwin, fasten your seatbelts.

Prey **Prey** **Prey**

Predator

Today, you lead. Not unlike every other day, but even more so now that you're driving the Lexus Coupe. Without question, the industry-anointed ruler of all sport coupes, the SC effortlessly presides over every intersection it passes, every on-ramp it encounters, every freeway it travels. Make no mistake, this ruler of all things paved doesn't meekly hold its own. Its sleek lines and soulful engine hold all others

Democracy EXISTS EVERYWHERE IN THIS COUNTRY BUT THE HIGHWAYS at bay. After all, on the interstate only the strong survive, or more to the point, flourish. This is a truth you know well. You have likely found yourself looking back on the pack, alone, with an unobstructed view of what lies ahead. And now, the opportunity to widen this gap. Go forward then. Take your rightful place behind the wheel. You have just been crowned the ruler of a vast and powerful kingdom - the road.

SONOMA SLS
Sonoma Regular Cab
2WD SLS in
SONOMA SLS
Apple Red,
shown with available equipment
SONOMA SLS

1997 SONOMA BY GMC

(this and following spread)
Design Firm:
SHR Perceptual Management
Art Director, Designer: Dennis Merritt
Photographer: Bob Williams
Copywriter: Gary Spedoske
Client: GMC

THE CHOICES GO ON AND ON, BUT THEN, WE WARNED
YOU SONOMA IS VERSATILE. SO HERE'S SOME MORE
AVAILABLE EQUIPMENT, ACCESSORIES, WHEELS AND ON AND ON.

COOL
COOL
COOL
COOL
COOL
COOL

STUFF!

WITH A DEALER-INSTALLED TRAILERING PACKAGE, YOU CAN LOAD UP A JET SKI OR A BOAT OR WHATEVER. SONOMA CAN PULL IT OFF.

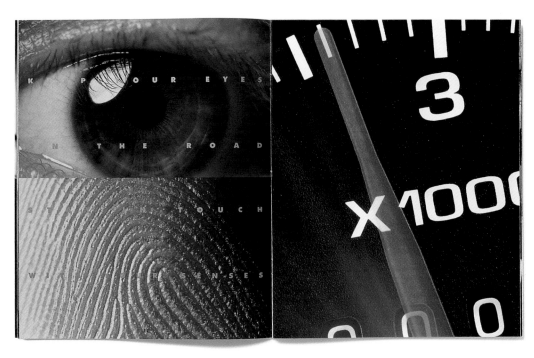

By the time you can say, "I'm outta here," you're outta there — with Sonoma's two available V6 engines. There's the powerful Vortec 4300 LF6 and the even more powerful Vortec 4300 L35, with up to 190 horsepower. Both include a list of long-life components, so there's no scheduled tune-up for 100,000 miles. Sonoma has a base payload capacity up to 1509 pounds, and a trailering capacity up to 5500 pounds. In other words, it hauls. The 2.2L four-cylinder engine, standard on 2WD Sonomas, is a potent force unto itself.

Be forewarned — there are some pickups that talk ABS but only have it on two wheels. Sonoma, on the other hand, has a four-wheel antilock braking system that helps you maintain directional stability, even when you have to break harder than usual. This is important in a pickup like Sonoma that has to be versatile enough to transport you, work for you and show you a good time.

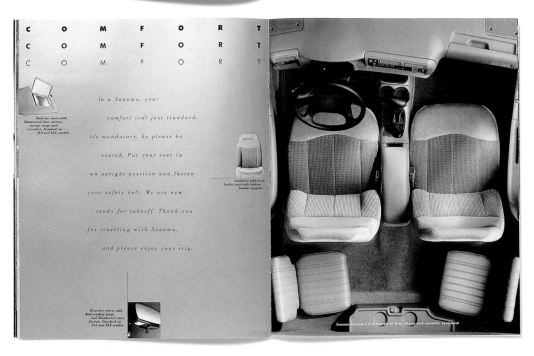

In a Sonoma, your comfort isn't just standard, it's mandatory. So please be seated. Put your seat in an upright position and fasten your safety belt. We are now ready for takeoff. Thank you for traveling with Sonoma, and please enjoy your trip.

GEAR RATIOS

Transmission Type	5-speed manual	4-speed ECT	4-speed ECT-i	6-speed manual
1st	3.285	2.804	2.804	3.827
2nd	1.894	1.531	1.531	2.360
3rd	1.275	1.000	1.000	1.685
4th	1.000	0.705	0.753	1.312
5th	0.793	N/A	N/A	1.000
6th	N/A	N/A	N/A	0.793
Reverse	3.768	2.393	2.393	3.249
Differential ratio	4.273	4.273	3.266	3.133

The Supra Turbo's 24-valve, sequential twin-turbocharged inline-6 develops 320 hp @ 5,600 rpm and 315 lb.-ft. of torque at 4,000 rpm. And most of that torque occurs at less than 3,200 rpm, so off-idle throttle response is spectacular.

The Getrag/Toyota 6-speed manual overdrive features short, positive shifter throws and its close gear ratios minimize power loss between shifts.

Front and rear double-wishbone suspension is rigid for optimum handling and road feel. Rate tuner lateral links and angled trailing links help Supra pull an astonishing 0.94g on the skid pad.*

The Turbo's ABS brakes feature large 12.6" vented discs for quick, fade-resistant stops, and a linear G sensor improves braking when cornering.

Sticky, super-wide, speed-rated radials complement quick power rack-and-pinion steering and tight suspension for "slot-car" handling.

Dramatic styling looks great and performs as well — the graceful air foil aids in front of the rear wheels help cool the massive rear brakes and differential.

Big power requires big safety and the Supra Limited Edition definitely has both. ABS brakes and incredibly responsive engines, steering and suspension help you avoid trouble. And when that's not possible, it's nice to know that you have side-door impact beams, dual air bags,* padded interior panels and front and rear crumple zones. Cutting-edge technology gleams throughout. Supra's handling is predictable and precise, and its massive vented disc brakes respond with a no-fade 60-0 mph stopping distance of only 120 ft.* The result? You're in charge.

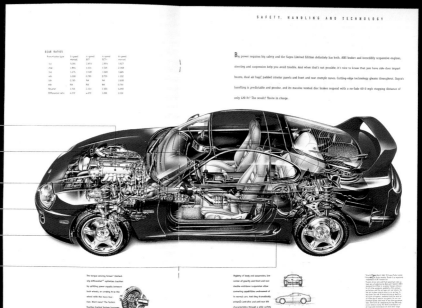

The torque-sensing Torsen® limited-slip differential* optimizes traction by splitting power equally between both wheels, or sending it to the wheel with the most traction. Want more? The Turbo's Traction Control System improves acceleration by limiting wheelspin when traction is poor.

Rigidity of body and suspension, low center of gravity and front and rear double-wishbone suspension allow cornering capabilities undreamed of in normal cars. And they dramatically enhance anti-dive and anti-lock ABS characteristics through a wide variety of performance maneuvers.

11

4Runner Limited shown in Desert Dune Pearl with optional equipment.

Tacoma 4x4 Xtracab V6 shown in Black Metallic with optional equipment.

Table of Contents

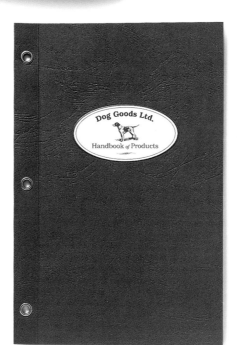

Design Firm: Pivot Design Inc.
Creative Director: Brock Haldeman
Designer: Jim Larmon
Photographer: Dimitre Photography
Client: Dog Goods Ltd.

Wide Line Collars

This line was initially designed for sighthounds who need extra-wide coverage at the neck. The two inch width tapers to ½", ¾" or ⅞" depending on size.

N⁰ 60-10 $44.00
Padded Collar: *Brown leather with Black padding*

N⁰ 60-20 $54.00
Star Inlay Collar: *Black leather with Burgundy padding and snakeskin inlay*

Wide Line Collar Sizing
XXS (12"-14")   SM (16"-18")   LG (21"-23½")
XS (14"-16")   MED (18"-20½")   XL (23½"-26")

Couplers

Our Coupler will keep your elegant pair of dogs in line.
- Brown or Black -

N⁰ CP6 (6" x ⅝") $24.00   **N⁰ CP9** (9" x ⅝") $26.00

Handles

Our training tabs are in a class by themselves.
The N⁰ HD-1 and N⁰ HD-2 are large enough for a two finger correction; small enough to be invisible to the dog.
The N⁰ HD-3, our newest handle, is designed to be grasped by the entire hand. Attractive padding affords a comfortable feel to hold your looklest canine friend in style.

N⁰ HD1 (5" x ¾") $12.00
- Brown or Black -

N⁰ HD2 (6½" x ¾") $13.50
- Brown or Black -

N⁰ HD3 (9" x 1") $26.00
- Brown Leather with Black Padding -
- Black Leather with Chocolate Padding -
- Brown Leather with Hunter Green Padding -

- for collar sizing please refer to page 34 -

Slip Leads

Our Slip leads are perfect for the household with many dogs.
They fit every breed and go on and off in an instant.
We offer varying styles and sizes to accommodate most any desire.
- Brown or Black -

Flat Slip Leads
№ 14-20 (6' x ½") $38.00

Narrow Flat Slip Lead
№ 14-10A (6' x ½") $34.00 • № 14-10 (6' x ⅜") $36.00

Laced Slip Lead
№ 14-30 (6' x ⅝") $48.00

Coursing Leads

Designed with the assistance of sight hound coursing
specialists; these leads function well. Large rings and 5' leads will
easily and quickly release your dog to the course.
A sheepskin lined collar adds support and comfort.
- Brown or Black -
№ CR1 SM, MED, LG $52.00

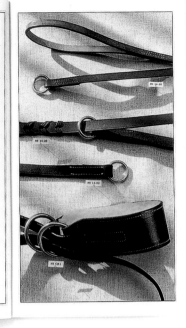

Our Coat Collection

Our coat collection is designed to function and fit well while looking great
in the process. To us, function means keeping your dog warm and dry.
We accomplish this with the materials that we use.
From Thinsulate,™ to Scotchlite,™ Ultrex,™ Supplex,™ Velcro,™ 100% cotton
and others, we create garments which work for your dog.

For fit, we provide ten sizes which, from our experience,
fit a broad range of shapes and sizes. However, if we miss the fit
of your dog, we provide custom made coats which
includes custom measurements and your choice of colors.

Coat Colors
Trim Colors: Black, White, Yellow, Gold, Red, Royal Blue, Navy, Spruce Green,
Silver, Beige, Kelly Green, Teal, Brown, Hot Pink, Purple and Cinnamon.
Cordura Packcloth (Superwarm Top Coat): Red, Royal Blue, Eggplant, Navy,
Tropical Green, Camouflage and Hunter Green.
Powderhorn Supplex (Warm Topcoat and Cappy Coat): Charcoal, Burgundy,
Hunter Green, Aqua Blue, Plum, Midnight Blue, Berry Red, Black, Bronze and Teal.
Ultrex Raincover: Hunter Green, Yellow, Red, Navy, Sunburst Yellow,
Black and Ultra Blue.

Custom Coats
Coats made to your dog's exact specifications are available
for an additional $10.00 charge.
Please choose your preferred coat colors (outer fabric and trim)
from the colors above. Provide A, B, C and D
measurements as specified from the sizing chart below.
Allow 6 weeks for delivery.

To Measure Your Dog
A Front center of chest to back of hind leg.
B Base of neck to base of tail.
C Base of neck to just above elbow.
D Around chest behind front legs.

Coat Sizing Information

Size	A	B	C	D
XS	14"	11"	5"	13"
JUNIOR	16"	14"	6½"	18"
SM	17"	14"	8"	21"
LONG-SM	19½"	16½"	7½"	21"
PLUS	20"	16"	9"	22"
M	23½"	19"	10"	23"
LONG-M	26"	22½"	9½"	23"
MED-L	26½"	21½"	12"	26"
L	30"	24"	14½"	32"
XL	34"	25"	13"	35½"
GRAND	37"	30"	16½"	36"

*"Tapered" coats are available in sizes medium thru extra-large,
in Warm and Superwarm styles. Please inquire.*

The Plaid Topcoat

Our town coat...but made to handle winter's rage.
Handsome 100% wool plaid, light weight
Thinsulate™ Thermal insulation and a 100% cotton lining,
together are a real winner.
Beautiful and warm! Handwash or dry clean.
{ Please inquire about our current available plaids. }

XS $50.00	LONG-S $58.00	M-LG $74.00
JUNIOR $52.00	PLUS $60.00	LG $80.00
SM $55.00	M $64.00	XL $85.00
	LONG-M $68.00	

The Superwarm Topcoat

The details of this coat are the same as the Warm Topcoat (pg. 27)
but is designed for even harsher weather conditions. The 150 weight
Thinsulate™ makes this coat suitable for wear in
temperatures between -15 to 20 degrees F. We use a tough
and durable 300 Cordura nylon packcloth for the
outer shell with a smooth and comfortable ripstop nylon lining.
- Eggplant with Teal trim -
- Olympic Red with Navy trim -
- Loden Green with Navy trim -

XS $50.00	LONG-S $58.00	M-LG $74.00
JUNIOR $52.00	PLUS $60.00	LG $80.00
SM $55.00	M $64.00	XL $85.00
	LONG-M $68.00	

T-Necks

Keep exposed necks cozy and warm with our fleece T-necks!
- Heather Red -
- Navy -

(12") $10.00   (18") $14.00
(15") $10.00   (22") $14.00
(25") $18.00

Design Firm: Tolleson Design
Creative Director, Designer: Steve Tolleson
Copywriter: Mike Coffino
Client: The North Face

(opposite)
Design Firm: The Leonhardt Group
Photographers: Don Mason, Doug Dukane, Tom King
Copywriter: Mark Popich
Client: O'Brien

Technical Outerwear
expedition system

Thanks to the revolutionary Gore-Tex 3-ply fabric process you don't need the extra weight of a lining.

Kichatna Jacket
Made of Gore-Tex 3-ply fabric that is fully seam-sealed and designed with multiple storm flaps, a unique ergonomic curved hood, one-hand adjustable drawcords, and venting features designed around the movements of alpine climbing, the Kichatna Jacket is one of the most functional and storm-proof garments we've ever made. It is the purest expression of our no-nonsense, technical design philosophy. Among its many technical features are articulated sleeves and our durable outer multi-position underarm zip.

Shell: Gore-Tex 3-ply Fabric with Lightweight Nylon Ripstop and Supplex® Taslan

The Kichatna Bib's two chest pockets are set high so they can be used when wearing a harness.

Kichatna Bib
Simple, functional and storm-proof, the Kichatna Bib with Gore-Tex 3-ply fabric was designed for extreme mountaineering and ice climbing. It features a rear slit-hole zipper and accessible leg zippers that allow ventilation in a variety of climbing positions. Tough Supplex Taslan fabric are used in high abrasion areas of the Bib's articulated knees provide freedom of movement and the integrated inner powder cuffs help keep snow from entering your boots.

Shell: Gore-Tex 3-ply Fabric with Lightweight Nylon Ripstop and Supplex Taslan

Conrad Anker rope in off a steep ice climb in Rifle, Colorado. Photo: Jay Smith

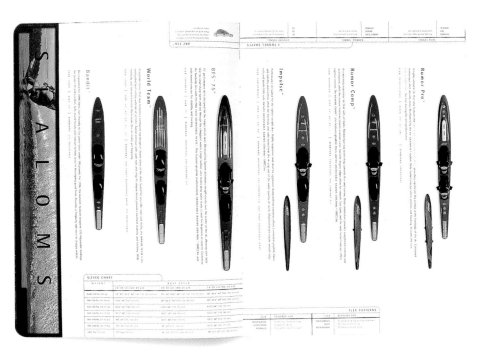

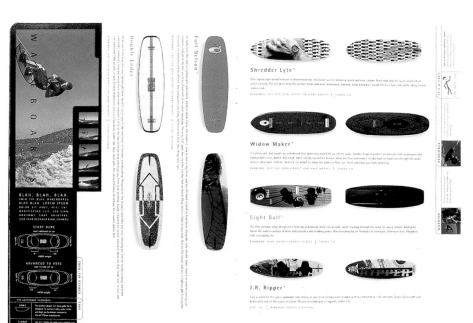

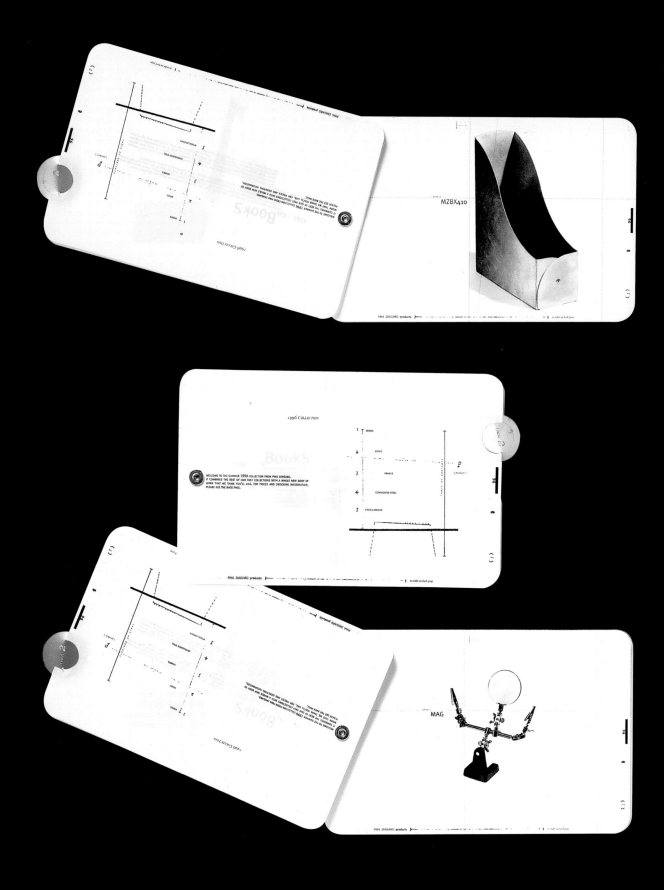

hans rey -
extreme mountain biker
(machu picchu peru)

As you go up the mountain, the distance between you and the rest of the world grows in more ways than one.
The reward for climbing to the top? The ride down. Sliding back on the seat a bit, gravity pulls you.
The ground underneath jolts your body. Rocks and stumps blur by.
A mountain bike doesn't have vocal cords. It's your job to do the screaming.

mountain biking

CYCLING '97

(opposite)
Design Firm: Jennifer
Sterling Design
Art Director, Designer:
Jennifer Sterling
Photographer: David Magnusson
Copywriter: Tim Mullen
Client: Pina Zangara

(this page)
Design Firm:
Sanmann Hammer &
Roske GmbH
Creative Director:
Bernd Sanmann
Client: Adidas

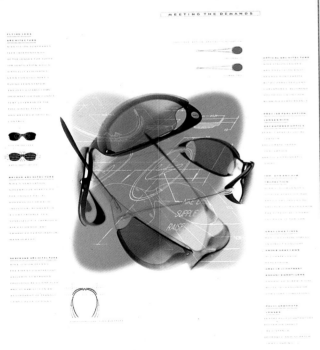

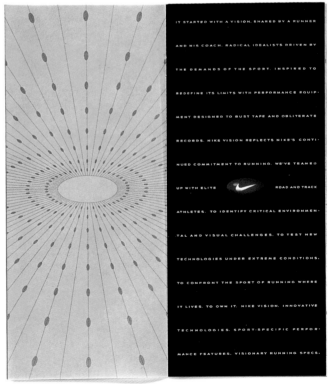

Design Firm: Nike, Inc. (in-house)
Creative Director, Designer: Jeff Weithman
Photographer: Gary Hush
Copywriter: Neil Webster
Client: Nike Inc. Equipment Division

1. We promise
to be your friendly
neighborhood global
communications
company.
Have a nice day.

A Promise

Design Firm: Goodby,
Silverstein & Partners
Creative Director: Paul Curtis
Art Directors: Hilary Wolfe,
Peter Locke
Photographer: Heimo
Copywriter: Paul Venebles
Client: Southwestern Bell

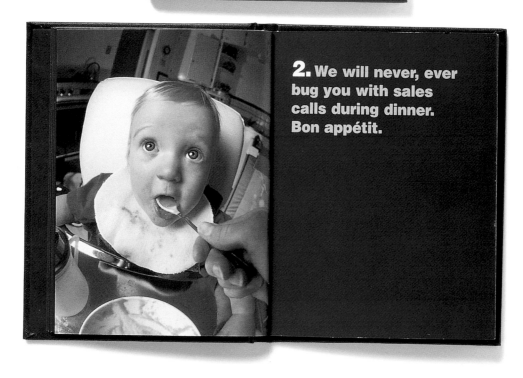

2. We will never, ever
bug you with sales
calls during dinner.
Bon appétit.

5. We will offer cutting-edge technology. (Hey, if NASA is using it, it's cutting-edge.)

12. Neither hurricane nor tornado nor flood will prevent us from helping the community in difficult times. After all, we live here too.

Our name is Southwestern Bell. Your friendly neighborhood global communications company.

Thanks for your time.

Design Firm: Hornall Anderson
Design Works, Inc.
Art Director: Jack Anderson
Designers: Jack Anderson, John Anicker,
Mary Hermes, Margaret Long, Jana Wilson
Photographs: Corbis Archive
Copywriter: Corbis in-house,
Matthaeus Halverson, Ayriss Advertising
Client: Corbis Corporation

(opposite)
Design Firm: Pentagram Design
Creative Director: Lowell Williams
Designer: Bill Carson
Photographer: David Grimes
Copywriter: Joanne Stone
Client: Pharmaco

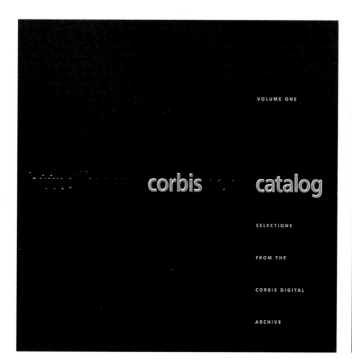

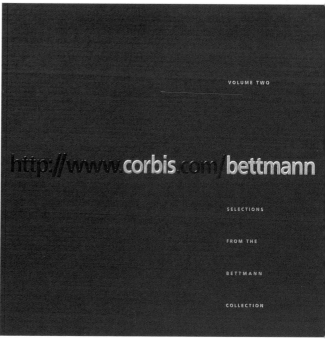

Design Firm: Hornall Anderson
Design Works, Inc.
Art Director: Jack Anderson
Designers: Jack Anderson, John Anicker,
Mary Hermes, Margaret Long, Jana Wilson
Photographs: Corbis Archive
Copywriter: Corbis in-house,
Matthaeus Halverson, Ayriss Advertising
Client: Corbis Corporation

(opposite)
Design Firm: Pentagram Design
Creative Director: Lowell Williams
Designer: Bill Carson
Photographer: David Grimes
Copywriter: Joanne Stone
Client: Pharmaco

Leicester Clinical Research Centre
Leicester United Kingdom

PPD - **PHARMACO**
INTERNATIONAL

Bioanalytical Laboratory
Richmond, Virginia

PPD - **PHARMACO**
INTERNATIONAL

**Pharmaco
At A Glance**

P H A R M A C O

**Data Management and
Biostatistics**

P H A R M A C O

(this and following spread)
Design Firm: Emery Vincent Design
Client: Workshop 3000

c   h   n

(this and following spread)
Design Firm: Emery Vincent Design
Client: Workshop 3000

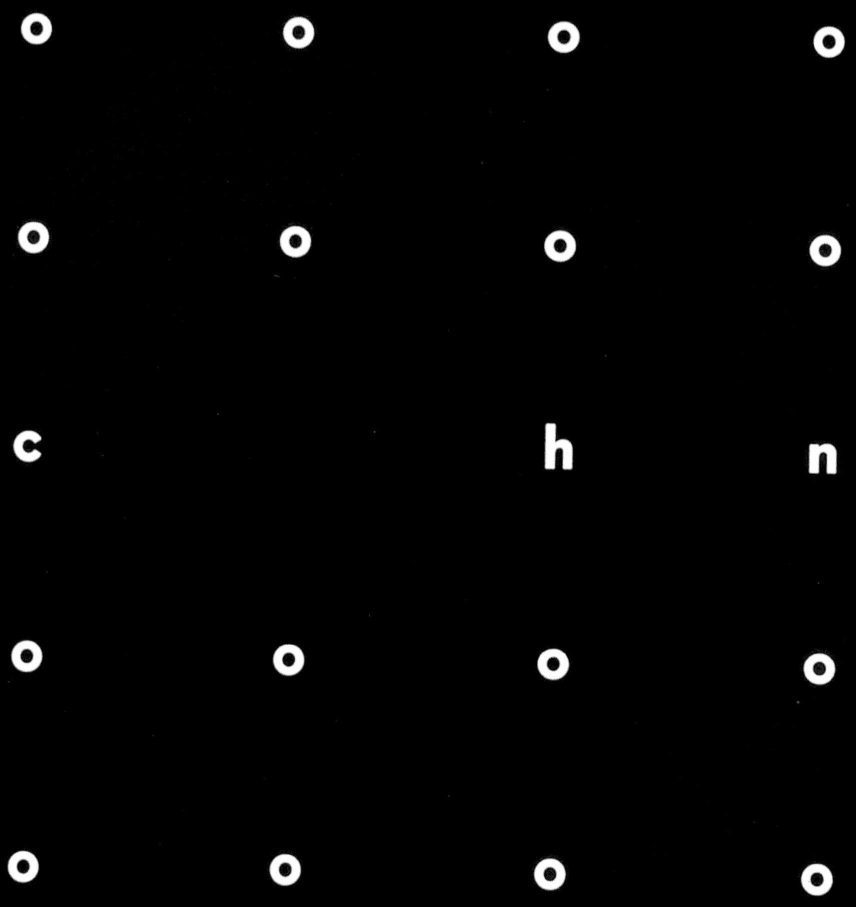

systematic reflections on a safe future

Way Past Real Anna Schwartz Gallery 1994 ● 'Way Past Real' examines the idea of the fake and the genuine article, and asks: what constitutes authenticity? what is real? what is valuable? In 'Way Past Real' she elaborates these themes rather than just posing the questions. ● One of the kind of this show is to go back to a real piece of jewellery – something that's real formally and typologically: a bracelet, something that's real in terms of its material: gold. The central questions behind most of Susan Cohn's work have an apparently identical in form, apparently identical in material and apparently uniformly produced. ● She chose the bracelet for several reasons. It's identifiably hers, like a signature; it's not a new form. So there are no distractions in terms of formal invention, and throughout her work, the doughnut has always been her experimental tool. The doughnut is also a production piece, and she wanted to explore ideas about the fake specifically, through a production piece. Taking comes out of mass production. And finally, the doughnut form is extravagant and luscious especially so in gold. ● There are four families of bracelets. Conceptually they all deal with authenticity, fakes, messages and coding, and vanity. But each family highlights certain key ideas. ● So many six bracelets constitute the family. Thirty-five of these are 24 carat gold plated and one is 24 carat pure gold. Of course, you can't tell which one is pure gold simply from looking: they all look exactly the same. But in thirty-five bracelets, five create the illusion of solid gold. Does it matter? And does it matter if you've got the real gold one or not? ● The second family of bracelets is gold anodised. Forty-four are made by the Workshop 3000 team, and one is made entirely by Cohn. How can you tell which one is the 'original', made by 'the designer'? Is it important? This family expresses Cohn's fascination with the way that 'fakes' or copies can be enriched with more cachet than the original – what happened with the fake Rolex watch, for instance. And also the idea of the matter creating the single prototype, which is immediately expensive and the identical production pieces, which are cheap. This touched on the mystery of the original. ● The third family is raw aluminium, just polished. But the bracelets are 1:1 conversely to look as though they are made of gold. However, as soon as you remove them from the lighting, the theatrical illusion is shattered. There are various ideas implicit here. How real is illusion? what is a star? (This latter idea comes out of observing how someone like Madonna has very cleverly built herself up to megastardom on a mixture of talent with large amount of illusion, glamour and hype.) And yet for all their simplicity, these raw aluminium bracelets are still authentic. Certainly they are not fakes. ● The next thirty-six bracelets have different surface treatments: all gold. Some are gold some gold paint, some gold dust. They are like all those fakes or copies which don't strive to replicate the original exactly – because it doesn't matter. They are happy to be copies and create the desired image. The bracelets do not pretend to be real gold: it's the most 'honest' family because of that. ● In 'WayPast Real' Cohn looks at where the fake crosses the line, where it becomes validated, and what is more real than the real. **Jackie Cooper** 1994

Selective Catalytic Reduction (SCR). SCR reduces NO$_x$ much like a car's catalytic converter controls automobile exhaust. In addition, scrubbers or fluidized bed combustion reduce sulfur dioxide (SO$_2$) emissions, which contribute to acid rain. And a baghouse — essentially a giant vacuum cleaner — removes nearly all particulates or dust associated with using coal. Together, such improved technologies and practices are setting environmental standards that would have seemed impossible in even less than 10 years ago.

Natural gas produces relatively few emissions and no waste byproducts. Gas-fueled combustion turbines emit hardly any SO$_2$ or particulate emissions. NO$_x$ emissions are carefully controlled — well below Environmental Protection Agency (EPA) standards — through state of the art control technologies, such as steam injection and SCR. Every USGen plant includes a comprehensive set of environmental control measures.

Preserving water quality of nearby streams and rivers is another important consideration at power plants. Consistent with USGen's environmental philosophy we make every effort to minimize each plant's water requirements. We also minimize — and clean — any water discharged from the plants. Several of our plants have zero discharge systems, meaning we recycle and reuse all waste water.

Where alternatives to fresh water resources are feasible, USGen taps sources for used water or waste water. For example, our MASSPOWER plant, in Massachusetts, uses cooling water from a nearby chemical plant for its water supply. And at our Indiantown Generating Plant in Florida, a 19-mile pipeline carries livestock and agricultural waste runoff water to the plant for its water supply. The result is a classic win-win situation: water for us, and a greatly reduced flow of harmful runoff into nearby Lake Okeechobee, one of the most beautiful — and ecologically diverse lakes — in America.

Air and water quality are closely related to land use in the design of a power plant. Land use considerations relate to protection of the land and ecosystem surrounding the plant. Wildlife, wetlands, and cultural resources are good examples. Deer, ducks, muskrats, bobcats, egrets, herons, turtles and even alligators have all been spotted

Air Flows.

Power plants use large fans to draw in air required for combustion of fuels. The hot exhaust from the combustion moves through  cooling, filtering, and vacuum-like technologies to remove emissions. Once the emissions have been removed, the clean exhaust travels up through the stack. The stack contains a sophisticated emissions monitoring system, allowing plant operators to make sure the air leaving the plant is well within air quality standards. You won't see any black smoke from a USGen plant. In fact, if you see anything, it's water vapor. Like your breath in winter, the vapor is only visible on colder days.

Design Firm: Rutka Weadock Design
Creative Director: Anthony Rutka
Designer: Priscilla Henderer
Illustrator: Tim Lewis
Client: US Generating Co.

KEEPING IT CLEAN

Today's power plant must be clean, and tomorrow's must be cleaner still. Communities not only expect it, but federal and state laws require it. And at USGen, we demand it of ourselves. In fact, our environmental stewardship has earned us the reputation as a company that will go the extra mile — beyond the minimum regulatory requirements. Several of our plants have set standards for air quality controls that all future power plants must meet or exceed.

With power plants, air, water and land use are key environmental considerations. Each plant uses numerous environmental controls, optimizes the land use, and reduces emissions created as a result of the generation process.

Consider coal-fueled plants again. We control pollution *before, during* and *after* coal combustion. First, the process of controlling sulfur emissions begins at the source through the purchase of low sulfur coal. Then, we use high-efficiency, low-emission burners. For example, CFB operates at relatively low temperatures, which helps control emissions. Once the coal is burned, we add other technologies to minimize the emissions to the environment.

Nitrogen oxides (NO$_x$) emissions are a major contributor to the formation of ozone and smog in the atmosphere. In today's power plants, ammonia is used in a process that converts NO$_x$ to elemental nitrogen and water. One particularly effective plant technology is

A glance at three stressful, yet not uncommon, business dilemmas snaps the issue into sharp focus. Imagine you're a chief executive or chief information officer facing one of these challenges:

"Up and running in 90 days? Are you putting me on?"

Your new HMO just signed a state contract to cover Medicaid eligibles. You'll go live with 2,000 members and plan to expand to 10,000 in the next 12 months. In just 90 days you'll receive a tape from the state with their names and become responsible for their health care costs under a total capitation program. You don't have an information system, your budget is tight and your time limited. But you don't want to settle for a short-lived product on the grounds of affordability and fast implementation.

HSD SOFTWARE AND SERVICES

What's your solution?

An easy-to-learn information system that can be up and running in three months, yet fits your modest budget. Furthermore, the system must be able to grow with your organization because you plan to expand into the commercial marketplace soon.

For just such situations, HSD developed **DIAMOND 725Q**, an ideal system for smaller organizations that need to meet the future now. Its streamlined set-up with pre-defined files allows it to be installed and operational in three months. The product fits limited budgets and requires minimal in-house technical support.

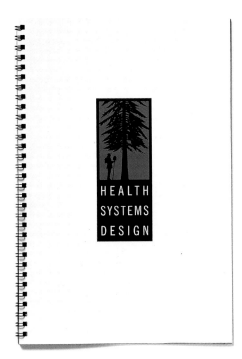

HEALTH
SYSTEMS
DESIGN

Design Firm: Pentagram Design
Creative Director, Art Director:
Kit Hinrichs
Designer: Amy Chan
Illustrator: Michael Schwab
Photographer: John Blaustein
Client: Health Systems Design

R HEALTH SYSTEMS DESIGN'S TOTAL SOLUTION
ecognizing that no single information system can meet the needs of all organizations, HSD developed the three separate Diamond managed care information systems mentioned in the examples above. They all provide core administrative functionality based on the latest open systems technology, share a common Windows "look and feel," and offer an upward migration path to accommodate growing organizations. We also are allied with leading vendors to provide additional functionality to our customers. Equally important, we understand that how a system is implemented and maintained is as critical as the system itself, and accordingly assign high priority to installation and client support.

THE ULTIMATE CHALLENGE
OF MANAGED CARE SYSTEMS

THE GROWTH OF
MANAGED CARE ORGANIZATIONS

Managed care information systems are larger and more complex than in many other industries. Their complexity is compounded by the lack of standards and business practices in the health care industry; the sheer breadth of the systems needed is an enormous challenge. In the future no single vendor will be able to provide more than a fraction of managed care's full information systems needs. As a group, health care organizations have lagged behind other businesses in applying available technology to their problems. Yet ironically, no other business sector has more to gain from the promise of technology.

Industries for the Century Ahead

The dynamics driving the industries of the twenty-first century are unmistakable. We are living in an age of extraordinary technological advances—particularly in the gathering, processing and communicating of information—that are transforming our economy and society as radically as did the Industrial Revolution. A constant flow of innovations is dramatically changing both the nature and delivery of health care, and an aging population will only increase the demand for such services. Increasing economic prosperity and a rapidly expanding middle class worldwide are creating a vast market for American goods and services, with media and entertainment products ranking high among them.

Technology, Health Care, Communications, and Media/Entertainment: these are the industries that will shape and lead the economy well into the next century, presenting both investors and entrepreneurs with their greatest opportunities.

11

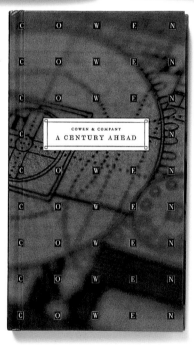

COWEN & COMPANY
A CENTURY AHEAD

Design Firm: Pentagram Design
Art Director: Michael Gericke
Designers: Michael Gericke, Su Matthews, Maria Wenzel
Client: Cowen & Company

Cowen & Company: Since 1918

Since 1918, Cowen & Company's success has come largely from our ability to target and develop businesses in which we are confident of building a significant market presence. This has been a characteristic of the firm from our earliest days, and has resulted in the present leadership position we hold in many of our core businesses.

Today, with approximately $154 million in equity capital and 1,600 employees in 16 offices around the world, Cowen is a major securities and investment banking firm. We have built an organization of enviable stature by entering new businesses through carefully thought-out and focused strategies, the commitment of every necessary resource, and patience in realizing returns.

Cowen's experienced, conservative management has been consistently successful in attracting talented professionals and maintaining the quality that has been a hallmark of the firm since our inception.

37

High technology has become the largest manufacturing industry in the United States.

Cowen's Technology research coverage includes:

Aerospace & Diversified Technologies
Aerospace, Defense Electronics, Diversified Technologies, Electrical Equipment

Computing Systems and Peripherals
Digital Media, Electronics Contract Manufacturing, Large and Mid-Range Systems, Servers, Workstations and PCs, Electronic Equipment

Software and Services
Information Services, PC/Consumer/School Software, Server, Tools and Enterprise Software

Semiconductors
Semiconductors, Semiconductor Equipment

Internet
Internet Technology, Internet Services, Internet Content

Data Networking

Twenty-seven Cowen analysts cover 179 companies within the Technology sector.

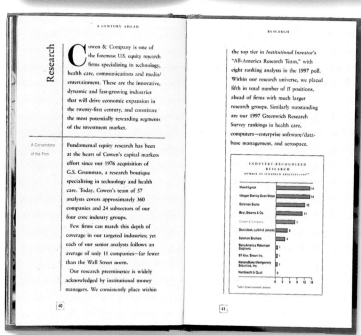

A CENTURY AHEAD

Research

Cowen & Company is one of the foremost U.S. equity research firms specializing in technology, health care, communications and media/entertainment. These are the innovative, dynamic and fast-growing industries that will drive economic expansion in the twenty-first century, and constitute the most potentially rewarding segments of the investment market.

A Cornerstone of the Firm

Fundamental equity research has been at the heart of Cowen's capital markets effort since our 1976 acquisition of G.S. Grumman, a research boutique specializing in technology and health care. Today, Cowen's team of 57 analysts covers approximately 360 companies and 24 subsectors of our four core industry groups.

Few firms can match this depth of coverage in our targeted industries; yet each of our senior analysts follows an average of only 11 companies—far fewer than the Wall Street norm.

Our research preeminence is widely acknowledged by institutional money managers. We consistently place within

40

RESEARCH

the top tier in *Institutional Investor*'s "All-America Research Team," with eight ranking analysts in the 1997 poll. Within our research universe, we placed fifth in total number of 11 positions, ahead of firms with much larger research groups. Similarly outstanding are our 1997 Greenwich Research Survey rankings in health care, computers—enterprise software/database management, and aerospace.

INDUSTRY-RECOGNIZED RESEARCH
NUMBER OF RANKED ANALYSTS—1997

Merrill Lynch	14
Morgan Stanley Dean Witter	14
Goldman Sachs	12
Bear, Stearns & Co.	11
Cowen & Company	8
Donaldson, Lufkin & Jenrette	8
Salomon Brothers	4
BancAmerica Robertson Stephens	1
BT Alex. Brown Inc.	1
NationsBanc Montgomery Securities, Inc.	1
Hambrecht & Quist	0

*Within Cowen research universe

41

New technologies in media/entertainment will expand our leisure-time options.

Cowen's Media/Entertainment research coverage includes: Gaming/Lodging, Media, Entertainment, Leisure Durables, Location-based Entertainment, Toys

Five Cowen analysts cover 31 companies within the Media/Entertainment sector.

HERITAGE BANK

A JOHNSON INTERNATIONAL COMPANY

sign Firm: Balance Design
signer: Scott Dvorak
pywriter: Keith Christianson
ent: Johnson International

Insurance Services

Strategic planning for what lies ahead should include a coordinated insurance strategy. At Johnson Heritage Insurance Services, we specialize in providing expert guidance through an extensive line of insurance products, including Auto, Homeowners, Life and Health. From our in-house claims coordinator settling claims quickly and fairly, to our expertise in executive benefit plans and estate planning, our goal is consistent: to provide thoughtful solutions for our clients through our creative planning, proven experience and competitive resources.

A solid commitment to local communities has made Heritage Bank a premier mortgage lender. With mortgage loans processed locally and quickly, our professionals enjoy the advantage of flexibility when tailoring programs to fit specific needs. To further ensure the level of service our customers deserve, we're committed to servicing each conventional mortgage for the life of the loan. This dedication to service and value is why countless families have chosen Heritage Bank to help them realize their dream of owning a home.

Complete Personal Financial Services

Whether the need is saving for a special purpose, borrowing for a unique situation, or simply enjoying the convenience of modern-day banking, Heritage Bank provides solutions. Choose from a range of checking, savings, and Money Market accounts, as well as competitive auto, construction, and home equity loans. Balance your checkbook or transfer funds between accounts with our toll-free, 24-hour telephone banking from anywhere in the United States. And, if you're age 55 or better, take advantage of the many benefits of Heritage Bank's Encore Club. These and other advantages are included in Heritage Bank's complete line of personal financial services, developed with the understanding that individual needs are as diverse as the clients we serve.

HERITAGE BANK

Heritage Bank began serving the needs of its local communities in 1970 when our founder, Samuel C. Johnson first opened the doors. The same family lineage that grew Johnson Wax into a worldwide organization has never forgotten that "the goodwill of the people is the only enduring thing." The philosophy of the Johnson family, of Johnson Wax, and of Johnson International, our parent company, remains as consistent as our commitment to exceptional customer service and meaningful community involvement. This unwavering dedication is felt in every community we touch and by every customer we encounter.

Design Firm: Maris, West &
Baker, Inc.
Art Director, Designer,
Illustrator: William Porch
Copywriter: Tal McNeill
Client: Deposit Guaranty Corp.

(opposite)
Design Firm: Graphica, Inc.
Art Directors:
Drew Cronenwett, Nick Stamas
Designer: Al Hidalgo
Photographer: AGI
Copywriter: Dan Lee
Client: Crown Wave

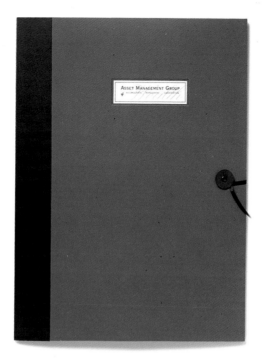

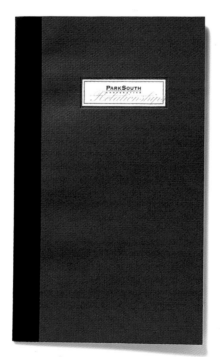

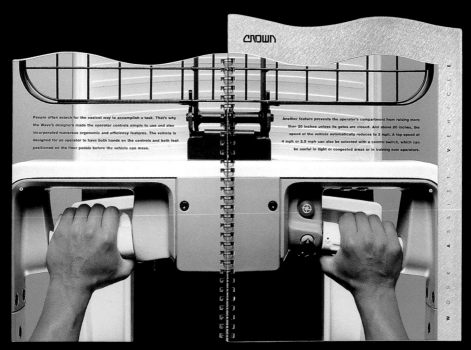

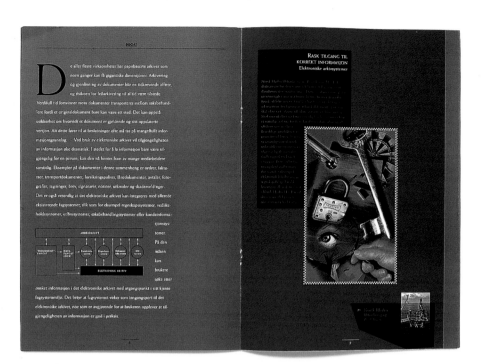

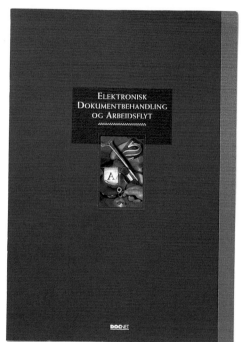

Design Firm: Bryce Bennett
Communications
Creative Director, Art Director,
Designer, Photographer,
Illustrator: Bryce Bennett
Copywriter: Anne Arden
Client: DocNet

(opposite)
Design Firm: Hasan & Partners
Art Director: Ossi Piipponen
Designer: Kimmo Kivilahti
Photographers: Marjo Tokkari,
Tony Bowran, Timo Viljakainen,
Mika Manninen
Illustrator: Matti Kota
Copywriter: Petu Pesonen
Client: Litoscan

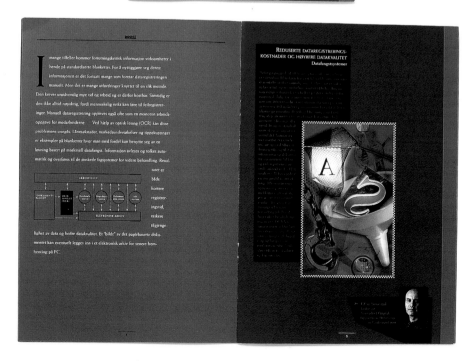

usein
aadeet
näkevät

sanoma-
lehdessä
punaista

MERKKI
TAVARA

"JOS ET ANNA APINALLE PARTAVEISTÄ,
et kai anna hyvää DUUNIA
KESKINKERTAISELLE REPROLLE."

Design Firm: Hill/A Marketing Design Group
Art Director: Chris Hill
Designer: Edward Tamez
Copywriter: Kevin Willis
Client: Global Financial Services

Design Firm: Larsen Design + Interactive
Creative Director: Tim Larsen
Art Director: David Schultz
Designer: John Ferris
Illustrator: Craig Frasier
Client: Imation Corp.

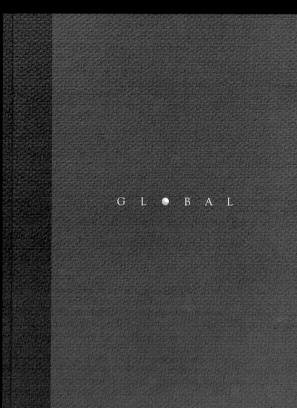

G L ● B A L

The Advantage is in the Service

IMATION

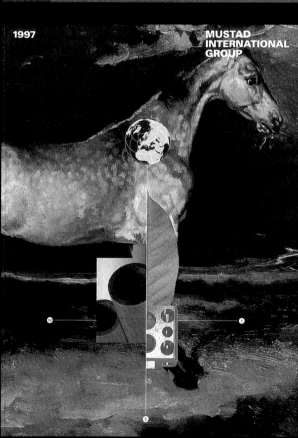

1997

MUSTAD
INTERNATIONAL
GROUP

EQUIFAX

EQUIFAX TELECOMMUNICATIONS
AND UTILITIES SERVICES

Design Firm: Saatchi & Saatchi
Creative Director: Yves Portenier
Art Director: Eric Fessler
Photographer: Nick Welsh
Copywriter: Roger Whittle
Client: Mustad International Group

Design Firm: Copeland Hirthler Design & Communications
Creative Director, Designer:
Melanie Pollard
Photographer: Fredrik Broden
Copywriter: Melissa Kamerly
Client: Equifax Financial Services

"**A**s soon as we find that a company is out of compliance—in other words if it hasn't resolved its unexchanged shareholders within our three year limit—we begin an audit. That means we can take possession of the unclaimed shares and levy penalties on the company. When we have the shares, our only obligation to the shareholders, if they ever come forward, is to give them the value of the shares at the time of the merger, which means all accrued benefits remain with the state. With the continued pressure on the state for more revenue, we've found that unclaimed assets are a windfall, so we're being even more diligent in searching out the companies that are not in compliance."

Fact No. 3:
More than
$35 billion in
unclaimed
financial assets
are currently
held by U.S.
state agencies.

"With the continued pressure on the state for more revenue, we've found that unclaimed assets are a windfall."

Rich S. Jeeter
State Unclaimed Property Administrator

The following story is true. The names have been changed and some of the characters are composites. This story could be your story.

Design Firm: Pentagram Design
Creative Director, Art Director:
Kit Hinrichs
Designer: Kashka
Pregowska-Czerw
Photographer: John Blaustein
Illustrator: Jeffrey West
Copywriter: Rita D. Jacobs
Client: Shareholder
Communications Corporation

The story you have just read is one of many where we, at Shareholder Communications Corporation, provided a client with the most complete pre-escheat service available. We begin with our research team and our state-of-the-art tracking database. We then follow-up with easy to understand mailings, investor-sensitive outbound telephone information campaigns and a toll-free "800" number. In every case, we ensure the highest form of due diligence.

Shareholder Communications Corporation provides this service at no cost to a wide variety of companies and industries including:

Public Companies	Banks	Corporate & Municipal Bonds
Domestic M&A	Lost Depositors	
Cross Border M&A	Unexchanged Stock	Called Debt (Full & Partial)
Uncashed Dividends	Account Reactivation	
Stock splits & Spin offs	Insurance Companies	Matured Debt
Mutual Funds	Unclaimed Policies	Uncashed Checks
Undeliverable Mail	Unclaimed Distributions	
Uncashed Checks	Lost Policyholders	

Shareholder Communications Corporation provides the complete service for undeliverable accounts: complete coverage, complete disclosure, complete resolution.

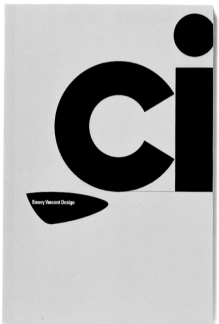

Design Firm: Emery Vincent Design
Art Director: Garry Emery
Client: Emery Vincent Design

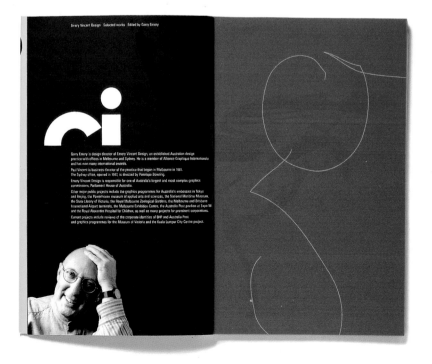

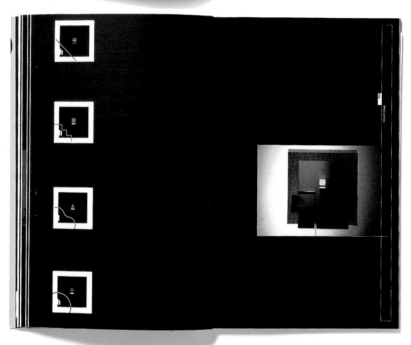

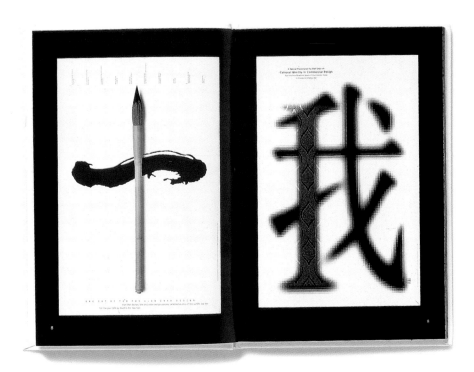

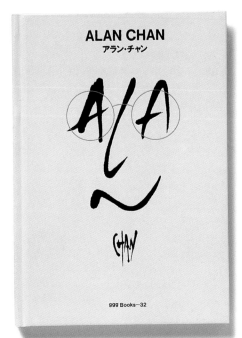

Design Firm: Alan Chan Design Company
Creative Director, Art Director: Alan Chan
Designers: Alan Chan, Pamela Low,
Alvin Chan
Client: ggg Gallery

45

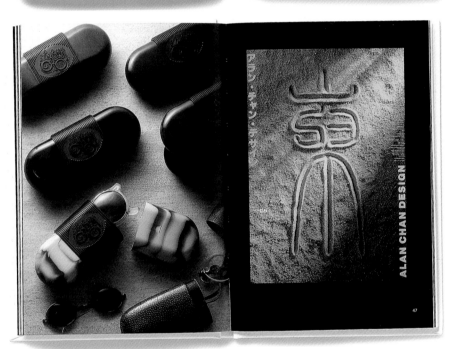

ALAN CHAN DESIGN

47

53

Creative Director, Designer: Copywriter:
Fernando Medina
Client: Arjo Wiigins Fine Papers

P
A
P
E
R
T
I
M
E

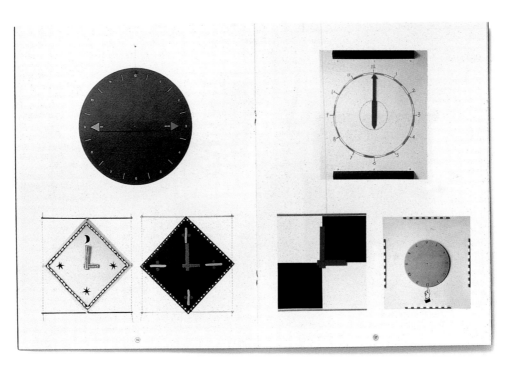

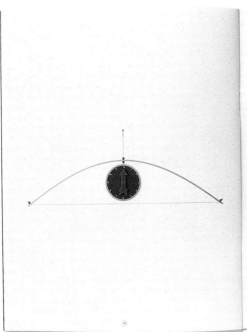

Fernando Medina

Born in the Andalusian town of Cadiz in 1945, Fernando Medina is an internationally recognized graphic and product designer. For clients such as soccer's World Cap, Ersol, Expo'86, NEOCON 22, Polaroid, and Expo'92, Medina has designed a body of work that includes publications, posters, identity systems and logotypes. He has also designed, in exclusivity for The Museum of Modern Art in New York, a collection of products that includes clocks, lamps, thermometers, and mobiles. "Papier Time", his most recent work, will be exhibited around the world beginning in 1996.

All of Medina's work reflects his profoundly curious nature, strong powers of observation, and a patient pursuit of minimalist solutions. His working process is equal parts child at play, philosopher in contemplation, and inventor at the workable. Medina defines and refines a concept until the essence of his original idea is realized through a balance and harmony of line, color, and materials.

"The pressure to innovate in design accelerates its evolution," Medina said in a 1992 interview. "Designers must balance the depth of their experience with the power of emerging technologies. But design is still a personal, organic process directed at the collective. It's not just functional or aesthetic problem solving; nor is it strictly a moneymaking activity. What we design on the outside comes from what we are on the inside and it also affects what we become on the inside."

Medina began his career in 1967 as an art director. In 1970 he established his own design studio in Madrid which was engaged solely in visual communications. In 1987 Medina and his wife, Monica, a close collaborator, founded Triom, an office dedicated to experimental work and product design. Since then Medina has lived and worked in Tokyo, Japan, Montreal, Canada, and Los Angeles, California. He currently resides in New York City. Medina's work has been exhibited internationally and his Peace Project is included in the permanent collection of the Chicago Peace Museum. Feature stories about his design have appeared in numerous publications including *Idea* and *Graphis*. Medina has lectured and led workshops at universities and at the International Design Conference in Mexico. He is a member of the Alliance Graphique Internationale (AGI).

December 1995

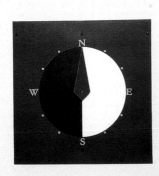

TAYLOR CONCRETE

Founded: 1929
Watertown, New York

A TRUSTED MANUFACTURER OF CONCRETE AND CINDER BLOCKS
"Quality is our foundation"

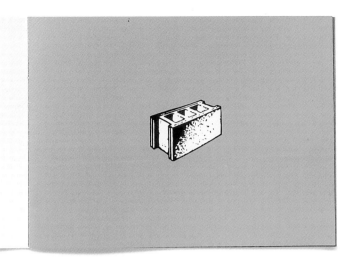

TAYLOR MEAT COMPANY

Founded: 1931
Taylor, Texas

FRESH, CURED, AND SMOKED MEATS DELIVERED ANYWHERE IN TEXAS
Meat says it so much nicer

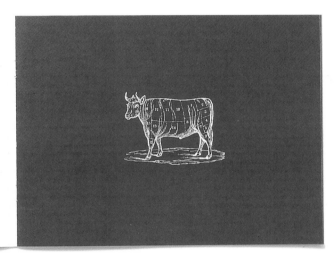

TAYLOR OIL

Founded: 1944
Sioux Falls, South Dakota

SIOUX FALLS' MOST DEPENDABLE NAME IN HEATING
"You can't beat our heat"

TAYLOR DESIGN

Founded: 1992
Stamford, Connecticut

SEASONED GRAPHIC DESIGN PROFESSIONALS
"Remember, bad design costs just as much as good design"

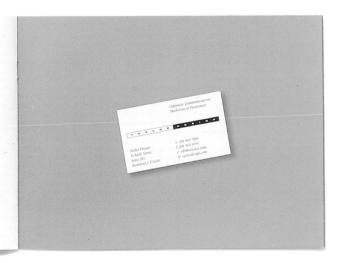

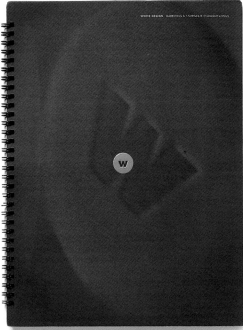

(opposite)
Design Firm: White Design, Inc.
Creative Director, Art Director,
Designer: Jamie Graupner
Photographers: Hacob Khodaverdian,
Juni Banico
Client: White Design, Inc.

(this page)
Design Firm: Mires Design
Art Director: Jose A. Serrano
Designer: Jose A. Serrano,
Jeff Samaripa
Client: Mires Design

Design Firm: John Sayles Graphic Design
Art Director, Designer: John Sayles
Illustrators: John Sayles, Jennifer Elliot
Client: Drake University

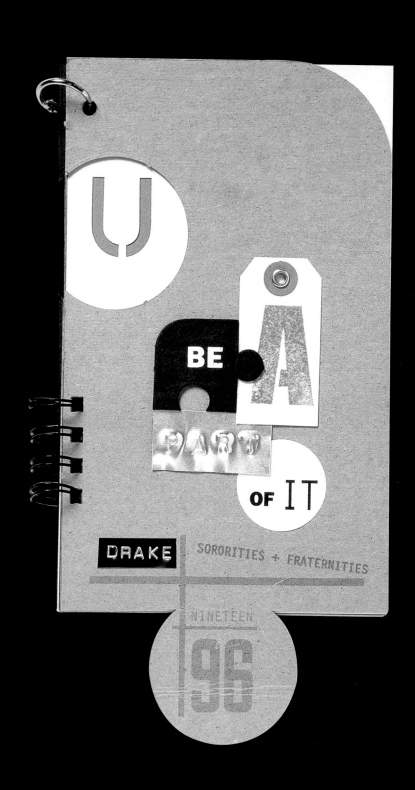

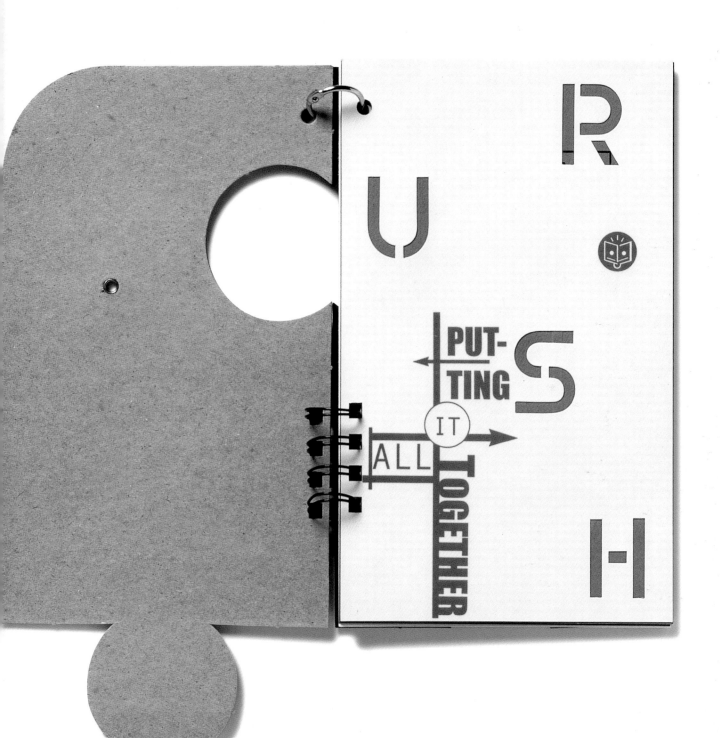

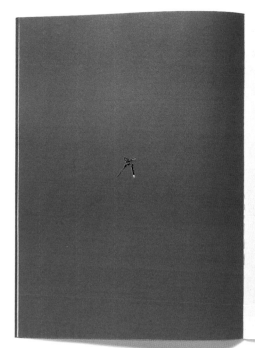

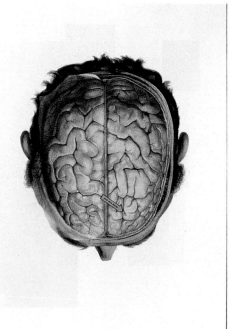

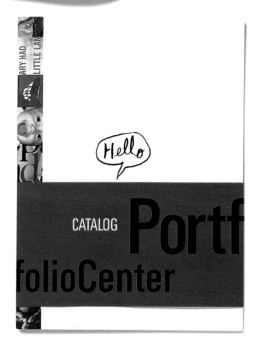

Creative Directors: Gamma Gatti,
Mary Anne Ritta
Designer: James Victor, Inc.
Photographers: Prentiss Theus,
Thomas Scherlitz
Copywriter: Sally Hogshead
Client: Portfolio Center

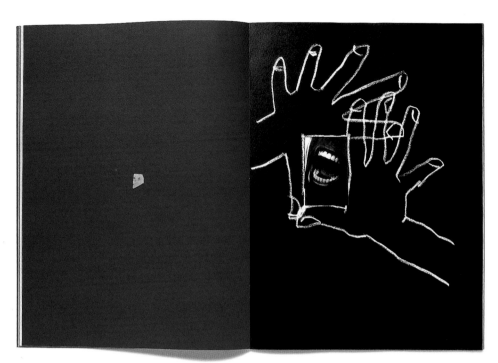

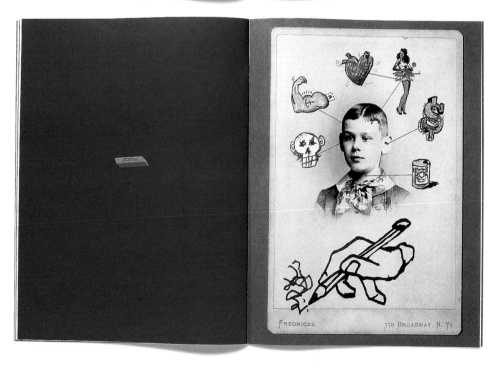

MARYLAND INSTITUTE
COLLEGE OF
ART

UNDERGRADUATE
CATALOG

PROGRAM OF
STUDY 1996—98

96
97
98

Design Firm: Akagi Remington
Art Director: Dorothy Remington
Designer: Kimberly Powell
Client: UCLA, College of Letters
and Science Development

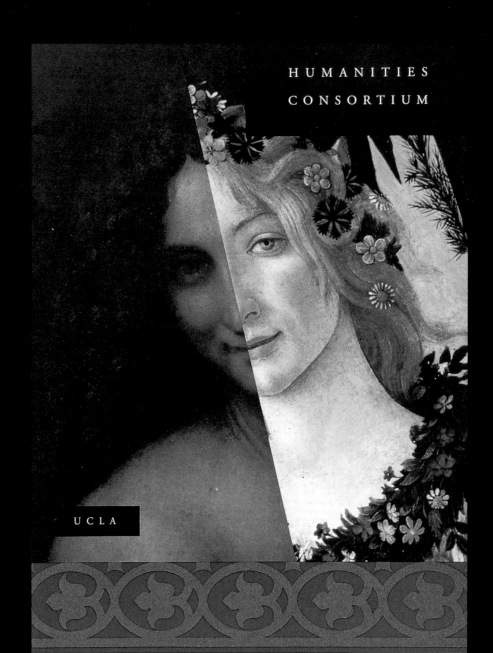

HUMANITIES
CONSORTIUM

UCLA

THE UCLA HUMANITIES CONSORTIUM

THE UCLA HUMANITIES CONSORTIUM

The Humanities Consortium at UCLA encourages the most widespread understanding of the cultures of the present and the past in a virtually limitless range of fields such as arts, history, literature, philosophy, languages, law, and ethics. As more future projects and programs cut across traditional disciplines, the Consortium will continue to attract more people whose interests lie even further afield, in medicine and the sciences. People from many different professions and occupations—including business men and women, community leaders, doctors, lawyers—come to the public events to share and enhance their interest in the humanities. And there is a worldwide audience for the publications that result from conferences, seminars, and research projects. The Consortium invites the whole of our community to explore the paths that lead to human fulfillment and accomplishment. To support the Consortium is to illuminate enduring human problems, questions, and achievements.

The goal of the Consortium is to nurture new ways of discussing and thinking about the most pressing issues in the humanities, to develop substantial debate across intellectual disciplines, and to forge new relationships between humanities scholarship and the public at large. The Consortium integrates the activities of three major Centers: the Center for Medieval and Renaissance Studies; the Center for 17th- and 18th-Century Studies, which includes the William Andrews Clark Memorial Library; and the Center for Modern and Contemporary Studies. Between them, these components of the Humanities Consortium cover a sweeping range of subjects, without regard for the conventional boundaries of academic disciplines, along an arc of time from the end of classical antiquity to the present.

The individual Centers have many interlocking functions, all designed to promote the keenest awareness and deepest understanding of the humanities, not just among students and faculty, but in the large and diverse community that is southern California. The Centers share a common purpose in supporting all the educational goals of teaching and research in the humanities departments.

With these goals, the Centers that make up the Humanities Consortium • organize concerts, conferences, symposia, colloquia, and workshops; • publish journals; • bring some of the world's best scholars to UCLA as visiting professors; • develop postdoctoral programs and award postdoctoral fellowships; • award fellowships to scholars who come from all over the world to use the collections of rare books at the Clark Library; • support, in general, a wide variety of individual and collective research projects.

As an umbrella organization, the Humanities Consortium coordinates and organizes, intensifying the activities sponsored by each Center and creating links with other areas of the campus. Although each Center has its own independent character, its own focus, style, and range of subjects, the Consortium has the ability to create a diverse and rich experience, for instance by promoting programs that transcend the limits of any of the Centers, by linking subjects and themes from different periods and cultures. Central to this mission is the Consortium Seminar, inaugurated in 1997, a thematic working seminar that brings together faculty, students, and postdoctoral fellows from all fields and periods, to explore common themes and problems. The postdoctoral fellowships have been funded initially by a grant from the Andrew W. Mellon Foundation.

It has of course become a commonplace to say that the population of Los Angeles is diverse. But that diversity leads to the most astonishing creativity. Here in southern California, as nowhere else, Native American, African, Asian, European, and Latin American cultures meet in an eclectic mix that can be tense at times, but which also allows us to understand how much these different cultures have in common. Our diversity produces rich opportunities for understanding the most deceptively simple question asked by the humanities: what does it mean to be human?

The Consortium does not just celebrate the past or preserve some idea of heritage against the ravages of progress. The purpose of the Consortium is to explore the issues that make us who we are, to investigate for example, the creativity that goes into literature, the fine arts and music, or the imaginations that have solved problems in the past, which can teach us how to confront the problems of today. The humanities are about life, and the Humanities Consortium tries to integrate and illuminate all the pieces of our lives that fit together, belong together, and need one another.

COMMUNITY PARTICIPATION AND SUPPORT

The activities of the Humanities Consortium receive support from the UCLA Humanities Council, a group whose goal is to provide private resources that are essential to sustaining the quality of research and teaching in the humanities. The Council is committed to sharing and extending the knowledge and values of our humanistic endeavor, to contribute to a richer and ever more creative intellectual life. It is one of the premier volunteer groups in the UCLA College of Letters and Science.

TO BECOME A MEMBER OF THE COUNCIL, AND TO LEARN MORE ABOUT IT, PLEASE CALL (310) 206-0609

COLLEGE OF LETTERS, ARTS AND SCIENCES

The College, home to more than 30 academic departments, is where you will find the heart of USC's liberal arts education.

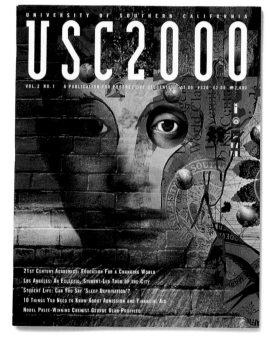

USC2000

UNIVERSITY OF SOUTHERN CALIFORNIA

VOL. 2 NO. 1   A PUBLICATION FOR PROSPECTIVE STUDENTS $3.00 ¥320 £2.00 ₩2,490

21ST CENTURY ACADEMICS: EDUCATION FOR A CHANGING WORLD
LOS ANGELES: AN ECLECTIC, STUDENT-LED TOUR OF THE CITY
STUDENT LIFE: CAN YOU SAY 'SLEEP DEPRIVATION'?
10 THINGS YOU NEED TO KNOW ABOUT ADMISSION AND FINANCIAL AID
NOBEL PRIZE-WINNING CHEMIST GEORGE OLAH PROFILED

Design Firm: Pentagram Design
Creative Director: Kit Hinrichs
Designer: Anne Culbertson
Copywriter: Sue McAllister
Client: University of Southern California

THEATRE

Students receive personalized training in acting, directing, playwriting and theatrical design—all elements of the collaborative art of theatre.

URBAN PLANNING AND DEVELOPMENT

Planning and development students at USC address the social, physical and economic issues of our neighborhoods, cities and regions.

"SAGE JCA COMPLETELY CHANGED MY LIFE.

WHY LIBERAL ARTS?

IS THE JOB THAT ISN'T TAKING ME ANYWHERE GOING TO RULE MY LIFE?

HUMANITIES

PREPARE FOR LIFE'S JOURNEY

With a background in humanities, you have a greater understanding of just about everything. All the creations of mankind—from art and architecture to literature and written history—are stored in this living museum. Studying the humanities helps you gain a better understanding of how we got where we are—and where we can go from here. Nearly all of our humanities majors continue in four-year programs. You can pursue exciting fields such as communications, law, medicine, politics—just about anything you can imagine.

PATHWAYS TO LEARNING

Sage Junior College of Albany

f o c u s

YOUR FUTURE

Design Firm: Rutka Weadock De
Art Director: Anthony Rutka
Designer: Lisa Catalone
Photographer: Bob Krist
Illustrator: David Plunkert
Copywriter: Joan Weadock
Client: Sage Junior College of All

LEAD IN EVERY DIRECTION

Sage JCA has over 50 leadership positions in student organizations, just as many as at most four-year colleges. But here you get the chance to take the lead in your first or second year on campus. You may want to serve as a resident assistant or orientation leader, or help with peer tutoring. In addition, there are social, civic, sporting and art events to organize, promote, and enjoy!

Sage JCA is about real life. Here—in your first two years—you'll have a chance to try all kinds of things, to work with other students to accomplish something great, and to see yourself as having unlimited possibilities. Often these experiences help you find your ideal career, or steer you toward a course of study you might have overlooked. Sage JCA helps you discover what you can do.

[STUDENT ORGANIZATIONS]		[INTERCOLLEGIATE ATHLETICS]	[ACTIVITIES]
American Society of Interior Designers (ASID)	Legal Studies Club	Member of the National Junior Collegiate Athletic Association (NJCAA), Division I Region III	Activities Fair
Art Club	Paint and Sketch Club		Career Day
Black and Latin Student Alliance (BALSA)	Peer Education Team	Sage JCA teams are called the "SABRES":	Earth Day
Black Roses Choir	Phi Theta Kappa (National Honors Fraternity)	Men's Basketball	Holiday Party
Circle V	Philosophy Club	Women's Volleyball	Leadership Recognition Day
Delta Epsilon Chi (Business Organization)	Psychology Club		Peace & Justice Week
Drama Club	Residence Hall Council	[RECREATION PROGRAM]	Portfolio Day
Golf Club	Science Club	Basketball	SenseAbility Day
International Club	Ski and Snowboard Club	Jogging	Student Art Show
Junior College Activities Board (JCAB)	Soccer Club	Karate	Stress Abort Day
	Student Government	Volleyball	Wellness Week
	The Phoenix (Newspaper)		World AIDS Day
	Vernacular (Literary/Art Magazine)		

Stories
about being
on the outside
looking in...

the women's home

...and then
coming in.

Design Firm: Rigsby Design
Art Director: Lana Rigsby
Designer: Thomas Hull
Photographer: Shaon Seligman
Copywriter: JoAnn Stone
Client: The Women's Home

The bridge in today's society
from hopelessness to a productive life
is a delicate structure supported almost entirely by two simple,
but often elusive, elements:
self-esteem and
human dignity.

Design Firm: Wild & Frey
Creative Director, Designer: Lucia Frey
Photographer: Pascal Wiest
Client: Universität St. Gallen NDU

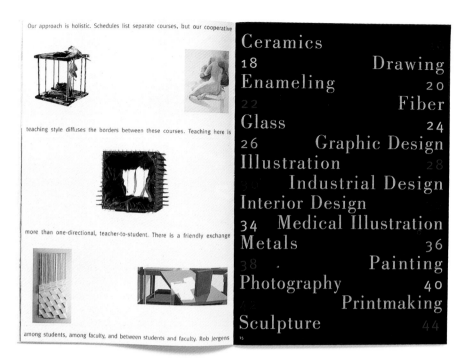

Design Firm:
Nesnadny + Schwartz
Creative Directors,
Art Directors:
Joyce Nesnadny,
Mark Schwartz
Designers:
Joyce Nesnadny,
Brian Lavy,
Michelle Moehler
Photographers:
Robert A. Muller,
Mark Schawartz
Copywriter:
Anne Brooks Ranallo
Client: Cleveland
Institute of Art

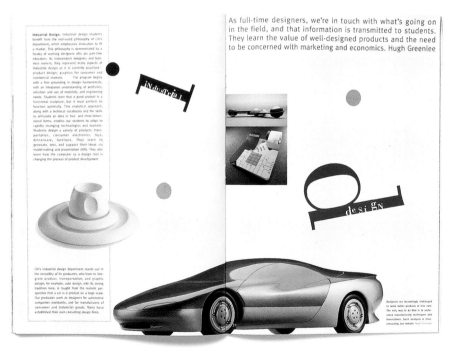

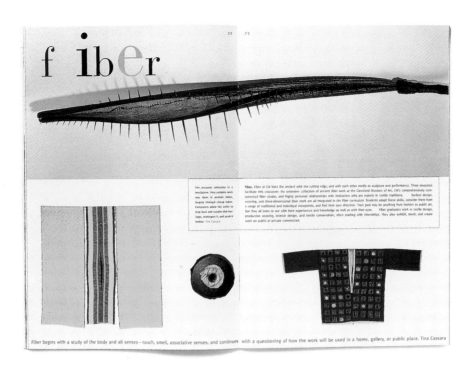

f ib e r

22 23

Fiber museum collection is a touchstone. Very samples work down to ancient times, largely through cheap labor. Computers allow the artist to loop back and reclaim that heritage, reinterpret it, and push it further. Tina Cassara

Fiber. Fiber at CIA links the ancient with the cutting edge, and with such other media as sculpture and performance. Three resources facilitate this crossover: the extensive collection of ancient fiber work at the Cleveland Museum of Art, CIA's comprehensively computerized fiber studio, and highly personal relationships with instructors who are experts in textile traditions. Surface design, weaving, and three-dimensional fiber work are all integrated in the fiber curriculum. Students adapt these skills, consider them from a range of traditional and individual viewpoints, and find their own direction. Their goal may be anything from fashion to public art, but they all learn to see with their experiences and knowledge as well as with their eyes. Fiber graduates work in textile design, production weaving, interior design, and textile conservation, often starting with internships. They also exhibit, teach, and create work on public or private commission.

Fiber begins with a study of the body and all senses—touch, smell, associative senses; and continues with a questioning of how the work will be used in a home, gallery, or public place. Tina Cassara

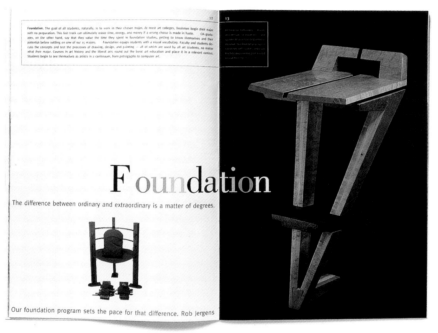

12 13

Foundation. The goal of all students, naturally, is to work in their chosen major. At most art colleges, freshmen begin their major with no preparation. This fast track can ultimately waste time, energy, and money if a wrong choice is made in haste. CIA graduates, on the other hand, say that they value the time they spent in foundation studies, getting to know themselves and their potential before settling on one of our six majors. Foundation equips students with a visual vocabulary. Faculty and students discuss the concepts and test the processes of drawing, design, and painting — all of which are used by all art students, no matter what their major. Courses in art history and the liberal arts round out the basic art education and place it in a relevant context. Students begin to see themselves as artists in a continuum, from petroglyphs to computer art.

F oundation

The difference between ordinary and extraordinary is a matter of degrees.

Our foundation program sets the pace for that difference. Rob Jergens

16 17

C e r a m i c s

Every student does something different. We don't have proteges, and there's no CIA look. Classes change each year, depending on who's taking them. We encourage students to use the information we present in their own ways. Bill Brouillard

To be a good ceramist, you have to understand two-dimensional concepts and express them in tactile ways, in three-dimensional form, for example. Drawing students can use their own information as clay instead of paper. Most students have more knowledge than they realize. Undiscovered resources abound, and they should be explored and considered. Realize what you know and use it. Judith Salomon

Ceramics. The ceramics department blends the contemporary and historical, collaborative and individual, two-dimensional and three-dimensional. Accordingly, ceramics students at CIA become well-rounded artists working in diverse styles. Early in the ceramics major, students concentrate on the vessel and pottery. They work with the full range of materials and learn traditional techniques of throwing, handbuilding, clay and glaze chemistry, and firing of gas and electric kilns. Later, they broaden their conceptual focus, refine their techniques, and adapt both to express their growing self-awareness. By sharing ideas, personalizing their sources, taking risks, and learning to criticize, they find their own voices. During their final year, students concentrate on their individual needs and build a cohesive body of work. Our exceptional facilities become especially valuable at this point: plenty of individual shade space, a co-foot-long skylight, five student-constructed gas-fired kilns, many electric kilns, a separate glazing room. Advanced students also learn how they will work alone, set up their own studios, and compete in the marketplace. Some go on to graduate school and teaching. Others work as independent artists, with work in galleries and museums nationally and internationally. An increasing number receive commissions for architectural and other large-scale works, while others become art consultants and conservators.

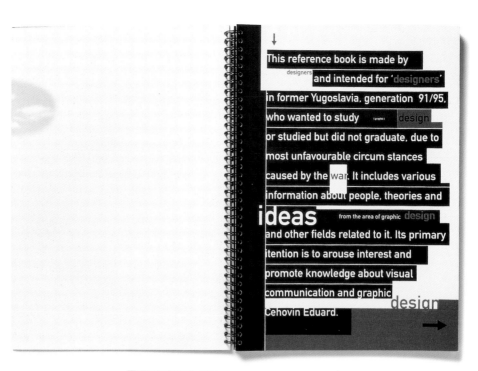

This reference book is made by designers and intended for 'designers' in former Yugoslavia, generation 91/95, who wanted to study (graphic) design or studied but did not graduate, due to most unfavourable circum stances caused by the war. It includes various information about people, theories and ideas from the area of graphic design and other fields related to it. Its primary intention is to arouse interest and promote knowledge about visual communication and graphic design Cehovin Eduard.

Designers: Bojan Hadzihalilovic, Dalida Hadzihalilovic, Slavimir Stojanovic, Tanja Radez, Darko Mlladinovic, Bostjan Botas Kenda, Lena Pislak Balant, Boris Balant, Eduard Cehovin
Client: Designer's Group

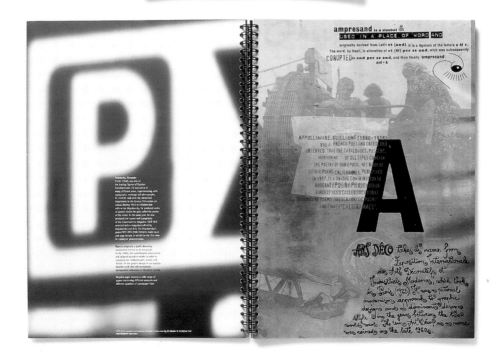

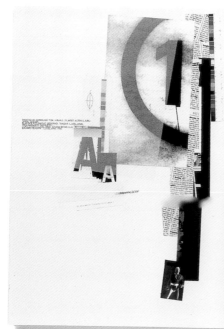

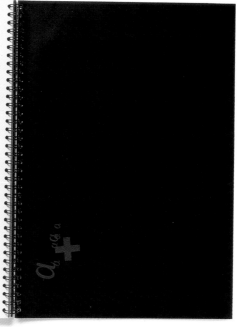

Design Firm: Pentagram Design
Art Director: Paula Scher
Designer: Lisa Mazur
Client: The Public Theater

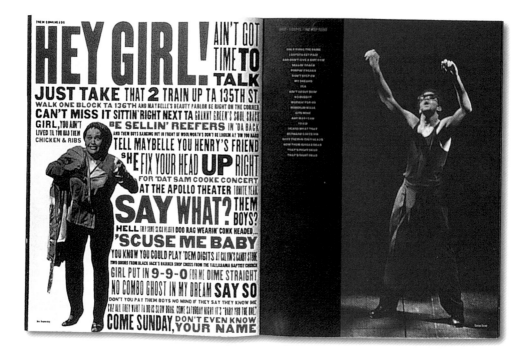

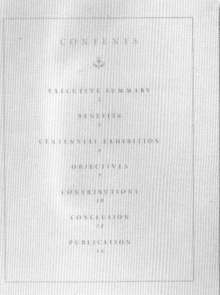

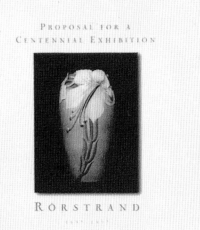

Design Firm: Socio X
Art Director: Bridget de Socio
Photographer: Noel Allum
Copywriter: Jacqueline Yoakum,
Eldon Wong
Client: Robert Schrieber

Design Firm: Siegel & Gale
Creative Director: Cheryl Heller
Art Director: Karina Hadida
Copywriter: Buzz Hartshorn
Client: International Center of Photography

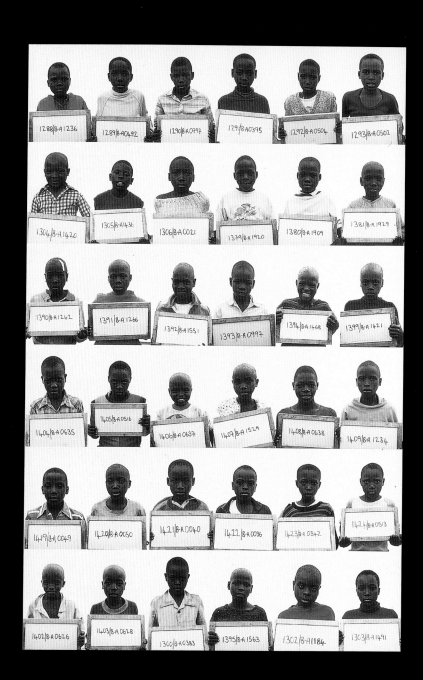

In recognition of outstanding work, ICP has honored Sebastião Salgado—one of the most important practitioners of photojournalism working today—with three Infinity Awards and three exhibitions in ten years, including, in 1996, *Workers: An Archaeology of the Industrial Age.*

In the past two decades photography has found its place in the worlds of critical discourse and collectible artifacts. It is now crucial to understand how photographs function within a larger context to reflect and shape culture. The concept of visual literacy—the ability to understand how photographs communicate ideas and also influence opinions—informs many of ICP's programs. Beyond the courses offered at the museum, ICP works with teachers in five public schools, employing photography to enhance learning within their curriculums as students make and use pictures in a range of courses. These programs have been particularly successful in teaching English as a second language and in helping students to develop the self-esteem that comes from mastering new aesthetic and technical skills. Our internship program enables students to continue their work and study at ICP. Such programs help us to reach young people and their teachers, using photography to provide them with another vocabulary with which to reflect on their lives, their neighborhoods, and the world around them.

As recently as five years ago, in the face of developing digital technologies, it appeared to many that the role of photography and its practitioners was becoming increasingly challenged. Just as photography's invention was considered the death of painting in the mid-19th century, so too has digital photography been seen by many to threaten traditional photographic values. It is clear today that although the new technologies present many changes in how we understand the operations of the camera image, they provide an enormous incentive to expand the world of pictures, making them more accessible. As the role of photography becomes more complex and influential in our daily lives, understanding the power of pictures is more than an aesthetic diversion, it is a cultural necessity.

Expanding ICP's commitment to new media, *Along the Frontier* traveled to St. Petersburg, Prague, Warsaw, and Kiev. The project marked the first multimedia exhibition by American artists to be shown in most of these cities.

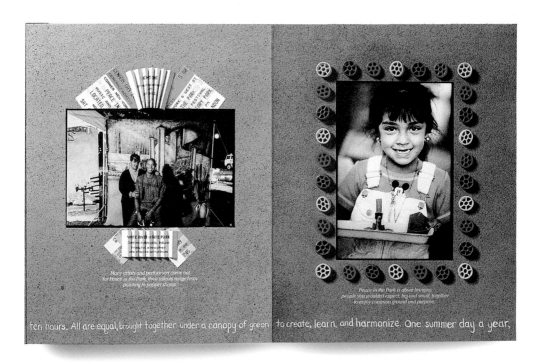

Many artists and performers come out for Peace in the Park, their talents range from painting to puppet shows.

Peace in the Park is about bringing people you wouldn't expect, big and small, together to enjoy common ground and purpose.

ten hours. All are equal, brought together under a canopy of green to create, learn, and harmonize. One summer day a year,

Peace in the Park

Agency: Young & Laramore Advertising
Creative Directors: David Young,
Jeff Laramore
Art Director: Chris Beatty
Photographers: Greg Whitaker Copy-
writer: Tim Abare
Client: Peace in the Park

Local and national bands, hand picked for their diverse musical styles grace the main stage throughout the day.

The Children's Pavilion gives kids a place to call their own by offering activities and performances just for them.

born from lips accustomed to parades. The peekaboo girl keeps her eyes wide open, waiting for jars of paint to open, murals

Design Firm: Principia Graphica
Client: Pacific Northwest College of Art
Art Directors: Robin Rickabaugh,
Heidi Rickabaugh
Designers, Photographers: Brian Kerr,
Robin Rickabaugh
Copywriter: Brian Kerr

Design Firm: KROG
Art Director, Designer: Edi Berk
Photographer: Janez Puksic
Client: Obrtna zbornica Slovenije

DOMAČE IN UMETNOSTNE OBRTI NA SLOVENSKEM

Prof. dr. Janez Bogataj

1. Opredelitev pojmov

Pojem domače obrti se je izoblikoval in ustalil šele v drugi polovici 19. stoletja, torej v času, ko so tej gospodarski panogi pripisovali velik pomen. Označevali so jo kot domačo delavnost ali hišno industrijo. Danes predstavlja domača obrt celo vrsto delovnih opravil in predmetov, ki jih izdelujejo ljudje na svojih domovih ali v domačih delavnicah za lastno rabo ali za prodajo. Vse do te opredelitve je izraz domača obrt pomenil kmetovo postransko ali dopolnilno delo, izdelovanje najrazličnejših predmetov na podeželju. Domačo obrt so opredeljevali kot paleto dejavnosti, ki temeljijo na tradiciji in so postranska zaposlitev kmečkega prebivalstva. Opredelitev domače obrti je bila torej neposredno povezana z gospodarskimi tipi našega podeželja. Danes je domača obrt kot sestavina krajevne določljivosti, torej podeželja (v najširšem pomenu ali pa tudi glede na konkretna okolja), nepomembna oz. ni odločujoča za opredeljevanje domače obrti ali posameznih panog. Mnoge panoge domače obrti so namreč zaživele tudi v mestih in drugih nepodeželskih okoljih. Seveda pa ima krajevno opredeljevanje veliko vlogo pri oblikovanju

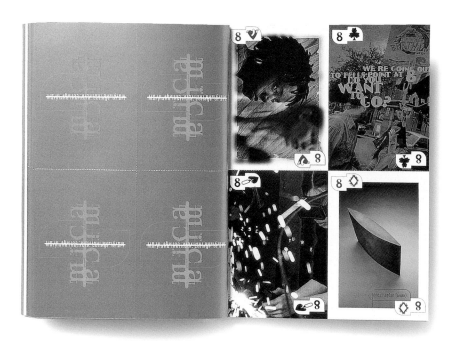

Design Firm:
Grafik Communications Ltd.
Creative Director: Judy Kirpich
Designers: Jonathan Amen,
Gregg Glaviano
Photographer: Joe Rubino
Illustrator: Jonathan Amen
Copywriter: Debra Rubino
Client: Maryland Institute
College of Art

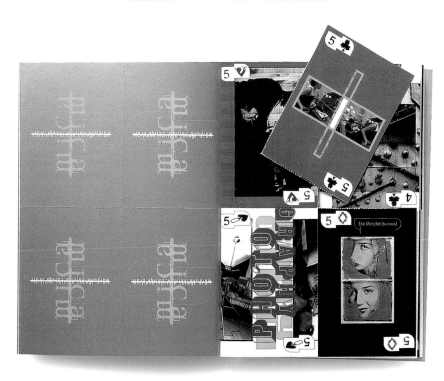

(this and following spread)
Design Firm: Neiman Marcus (in-house)
Creative Director: Georgia Christiansen
Photographer: Peggy Sirota
Client: Neiman Marcus

JOHNNY FARAH

STEPHEN DWECK

Neiman Marcus

THE

ART

how will you choose to tell your story?

OF

ACCESSORIES

Neiman Marcus

G.G. FIORENTINO

DAVID YURMAN

DANIEL SWAROVSKI

Neiman Marcus

MOSCHINO

MICHAEL DAWKINS

Neiman Marcus   SALLY GISSING   ACCESSORY ACCENT   NEIMAN MARCUS

SALVATORE FERRAGAMO   *Neiman Marcus*

ST. JOHN ACCESSORIES

M + J SAVITT

ROBERT LEE MORRIS   *Neiman Marcus*

Neiman Marcus   RICHARD TYLER

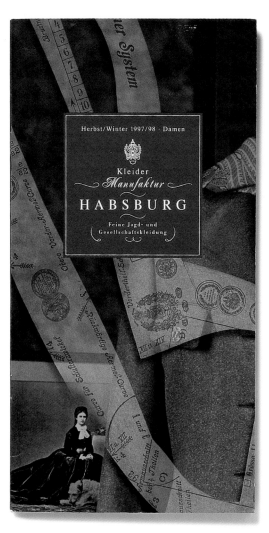

Herbst/Winter 1997/98 · Damen

Kleider
Manufaktur
HABSBURG

Feine Jagd- und
Gesellschaftskleidung

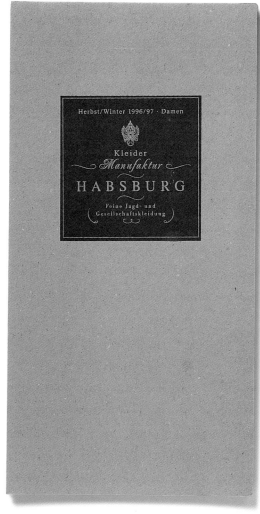

Herbst/Winter 1996/97 · Damen

Kleider
Manufaktur
HABSBURG

Feine Jagd- und
Gesellschaftskleidung

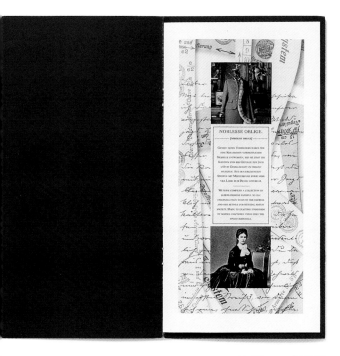

Design Firm:
Demner, Merlicek & Bergmann
Creative Director: Franz Merlicek
Art Directors: Franz Merlicek,
Max Jurasch, Harald Ströbel
Designers: Harald Ströbel, Max Jurasch
Photographer: Bernhard Angerer
Cover Photoillustration: Max Jurasch
Illustrator: Jürgen Mick
Copywriter: Karin Kammlander
Client: Kleidermanufaktur Habsburg

(this and following spread)
Design Firm: ZaNon Design Communication
Creative Director: L. Ganeo
Art Director: C. Zanon
Client: Belfe S.P.A.

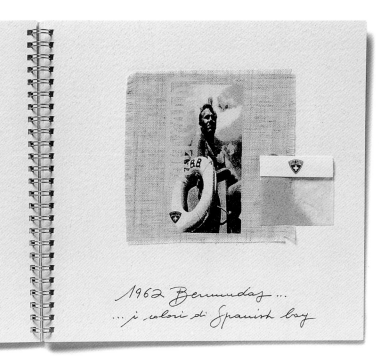

1962 Bermudas...
...i colori di Spanish boy

pomeriggio a Stanley Park
danne, danne in evoluzione...

...ho incontrato Marilyn nel 1962,
a Giugno. Je tempo prometteva...

COLLECTION WINTER '97/98

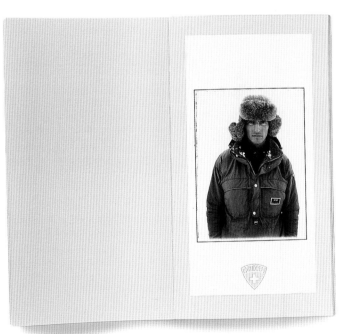

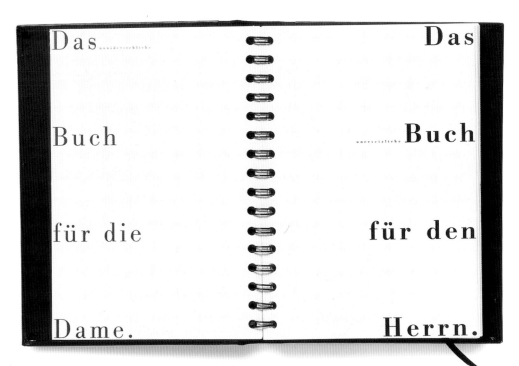

Das unwiderstehliche   Das

Buch   unersetzliche Buch

für die   für den

Dame.   Herrn.

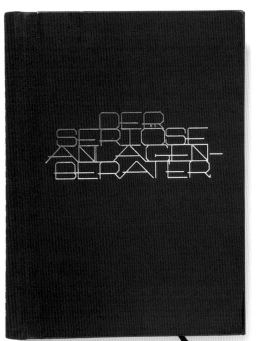

(this and following spread)
Design Firm: HEBE. Werbung & Design
Creative Director, Art Director, Designer,
Copywriter: Reiner Hebe
Photographer: Dominik Hatt, Francis Koenig
Client: Matthias Mass, Juwelier

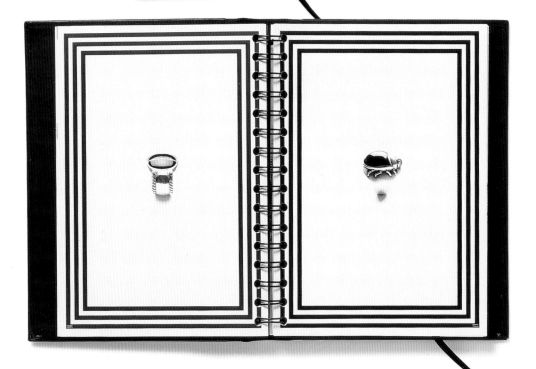

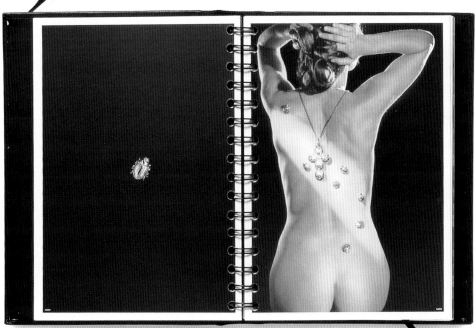

DIE KRÖNUNG DER HOSE.

Design Firm: Willoughby
Design Group
Art Director, Designer: Ingred Sidie
Photographer: Guido Vitti
Copywriter: Mara Friedman
Client: Lee Company

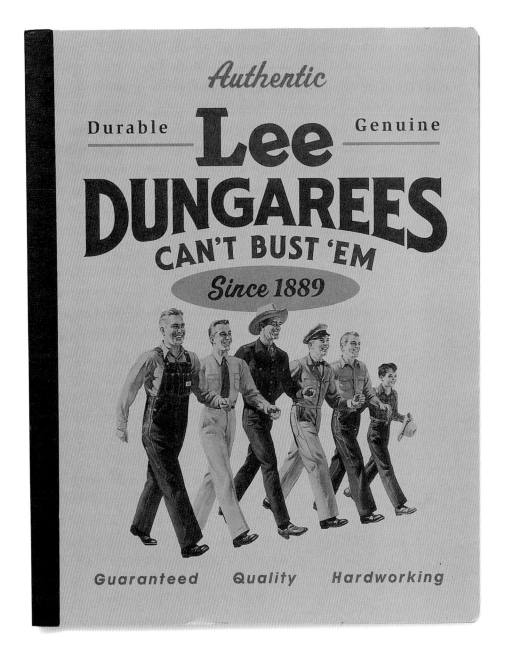

(opposite)
Design Firm: Bianco & Cucco
Art Directors, Designers:
Giovanni Bianco, Susanna Cucco
Photographer: Jan Welters
Client: Gruppo Imec

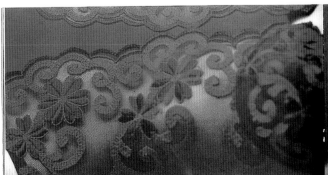

Jaro™

Exquisite

Snowboarding

Apparel and

Streetwear

Snow flurries scatter fiercely around the mountain. A dark sky, navy

blue and heavy with storm clouds whips against the soft, white

surface of the slopes. The only visible light is the gleam of fresh

white snow, silently reflecting the tumultuous rage above your head,

the early setting winter sun having already ducked down behind

the high crest of the mountain's top. The storm had moved in

quickly: you could smell the waves of cold air preparing to cover

you with millions of frozen crystals. You tuck your head in tighter

against the high collar of

your jacket, determined

to ignore the strong

winds, and continue to put one foot in front of the other. The weight

of your board in your hands is unstinating against the thrill of the

hike to the top. The expected adrenaline high of the descent to

the newly formed hit increases your pace. You wouldn't miss this

for anything. Alone and with only the swirling snow and the

approaching darkness, you remember why you are here. You will

always be here. The love of what you can do, the pure satisfaction

of knowing you will always be a part of this.

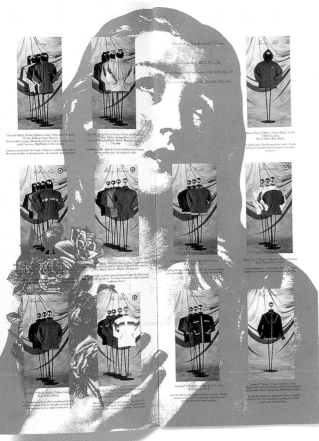

Design Firm: Poppie Design
Creative Director: Bill Poppie
Designer: Matt Tullis
Client: Jaro Snowboarding Apparel

Design Firm: Columbus/Italia
Photographer: C. Paggiarino
Client: Bally

B joyous

«Glamina». Small portrait shoulder bag in calfskin with front flap and Bally B jacquard lining. 6/7

«Glam». Large portrait shoulder bag in calfskin with front flap and Bally B jacquard lining. 7

B joyous

«Glamina». Small portrait shoulder bag in calfskin with front flap and Bally B jacquard lining. Shown in four colors. 16/17

B joyous

«Kira». Men's belt in calfskin with shiny palladium finish buckle. 12

«Barocco». Jacquard silk tie in geometric design. 13

Design Firm: Demner, Merlicek &
Bergmann
Creative Director, Art Director:
Franz Merlicek
Designer: Veronika Czak
Photographer: Jost Wildbolz
Frame: Bernard Angerer
Copywriters: Rosa Haider,
Annelies Litschauer
Client: Schneiders Bekleidung

Mein Liebster!

Ich überlege gerade, ob ich das M[...]
aus meinem Umhang bürsten oder
es noch eine Weile als Zitat um
Reise tragen sollte. Bist Du
geschmeichelt?

Jedenfalls werde ich es späte[...]
zwischen den Seiten meiner
Lieblingsausgabe von Oliver Tw[...]
pressen. Zusammen mit dem
Heidekraut, das Du in mein[...]
Haar geflochten hast.

Wie ist das Wetter in N.Y.? A[...]
wird es langsam kühl. Ich [...]
mich in mein Tartanplaid [...]
auf dem kleinen See. Als e[...]
Nacht wurde und noch imme[...]
Fisch angebissen hatte.
Vielleicht haben wir zu la[...]
gelacht. War es nicht vorge[...]

Paris / 53 Reiseta

Sabina / 24   Berlei / 25 INNOVATION

Design Firm: Searls Design
Creative Director, Designer: Kathleen Chambers
Photographer: Kop Brundage
Client: Kelmscott Farm

KELMSCOTT RUG: Thank you, Mr. Morris.

KELMSCOTT FARM™: A rare breed.

In 1993, we fell in love with an idea
that changed our lives – the idea of preserving
rare livestock breeds. This compelling mission
moved us across the country from comfortable,
suburban San Francisco to a remote hillside
in rural, weather-driven Maine.
It was here that we set about restoring an
old farm and importing rare livestock breeds
from England, such as Cotswold sheep.

KELMSCOTT SCARF: wraparound warmth.

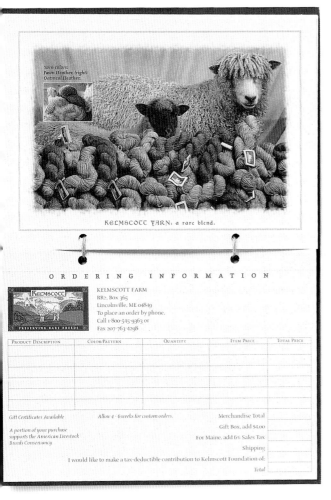

Yarn colors:
Fawn Heather (right)
Oatmeal Heather.

KELMSCOTT YARN: a rare blend.

ORDERING INFORMATION

KELMSCOTT FARM
RR2, Box 365
Lincolnville, ME 04849
To place an order by phone.
Call 1-800-545-9363 or
Fax 207-763-4298

Product Description	Color/Pattern	Quantity	Item Price	Total Price

Gift Certificates Available   *Allow 4 - 6 weeks for custom orders.*   Merchandise Total

A portion of your purchase   Gift Box, add $4.00
supports the American Livestock
Breeds Conservancy   For Maine, add 6% Sales Tax

        Shipping

I would like to make a tax-deductible contribution to Kelmscott Foundation of:

        Total

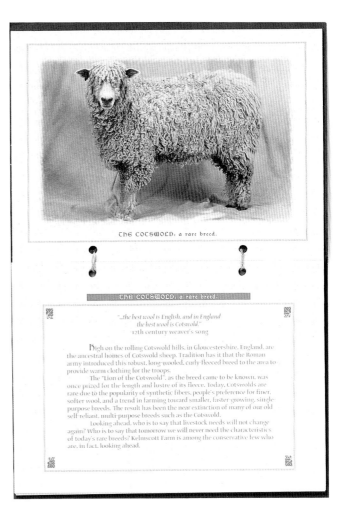

THE COTSWOLD: a rare breed.

THE COTSWOLD: a rare breed.

"...the best wool is English, and in England
the best wool is Cotswold."
12th century weaver's song

High on the rolling Cotswold hills, in Gloucestershire, England, are
the ancestral homes of Cotswold sheep. Tradition has it that the Roman
army introduced this robust, long-wooled, curly-fleeced breed to the area to
provide warm clothing for the troops.
The "Lion of the Cotswold", as the breed came to be known, was
once prized for the length and lustre of its fleece. Today, Cotswolds are
rare due to the popularity of synthetic fibers, people's preference for finer,
softer wool, and a trend in farming toward smaller, faster-growing, single-
purpose breeds. The result has been the near extinction of many of our old
self-reliant, multi-purpose breeds such as the Cotswold.
Looking ahead, who is to say that livestock needs will not change
again? Who is to say that tomorrow we will never need the characteristics
of today's rare breeds? Kelmscott Farm is among the conservative few who
are, in fact, looking ahead.

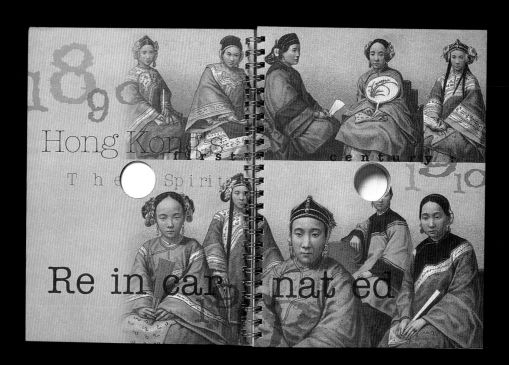

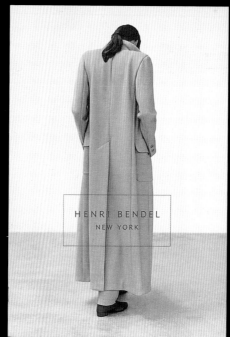

Design Firm:
Alan Chan Design Company
Creative Director, Art Director: Alan Chan
Designers: Alan Chan, Miu Choy,
Pamela Low
Copywriters: Lam Ping Ting, Ann Williams
Client: The Swank Shop

"Cool," he said. And
I kept on daring
him (with that smile -
captivating. I know!)
- to fight! Knew
he wouldn't. So
again I won, with
my hands down...

INDUSTRIA
COLLECTION

"if I could save
time in a bottle",
I'd save every
moment we shared
along with treasures
that added
to the beauty...
"if I could save
time in a bottle",
I'd save every
moment we shared
along with treasures

Calvin & Wilson

Fabrizio Del Carlo

VALENTINO

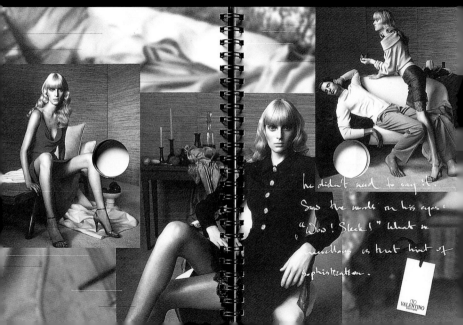

he didn't need to say it.
Saw the smile on his eyes.
"Wow! Sleek!" What is
marvellous is that hint of
sophistication.

VALENTINO

Design Firm: ZanOn Design Communication
Creative Director: Ciriano Zanon
Designer: Mara Biasia
Photographer: Claudio Mainardi
Copywriter: Ciriano Zanon
Client: GB International

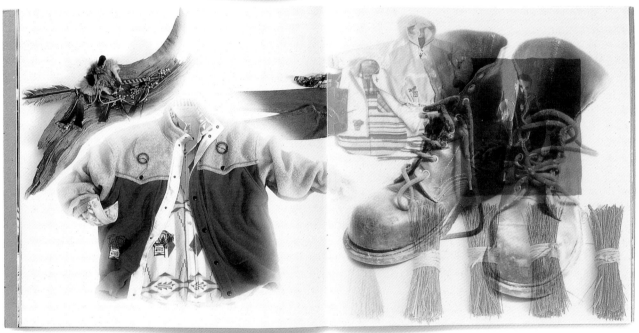

Design Firm: ZanOn Design
Communications
Creative Director: Luana Ganeo
Art Director, Illustrator, Copywriter:
Ciriano Zanon
Designers: Luana Ganeo, Ciriano Zanon
Photographer: Gianni Baccesa
Client: Stonefly Spa

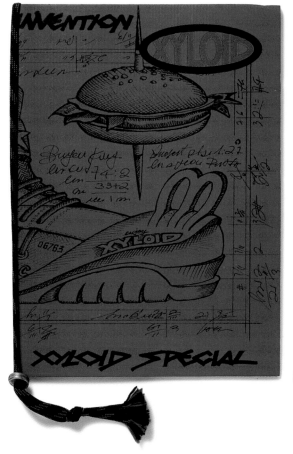

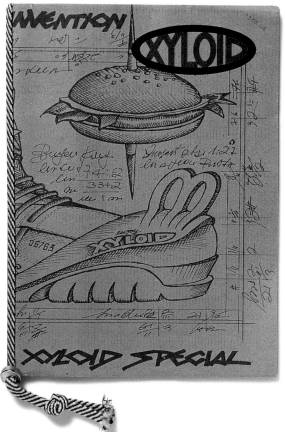

(opposite)
Design Firm: Hal Apple Design
Creative Director: Alan Otto
Art Director: Hal Apple
Designer: Andrea Del Guercio
Photographer: Sean Bolger
Copywriter: Mitch Werner
Client: Rampage Clothing Co.

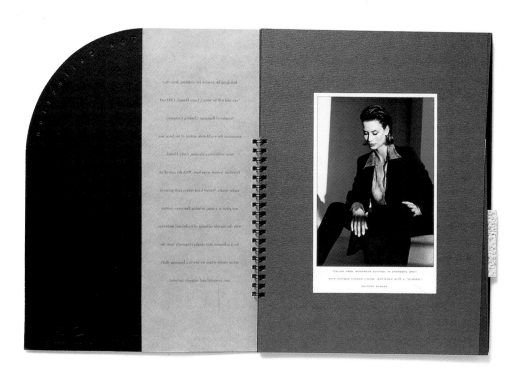

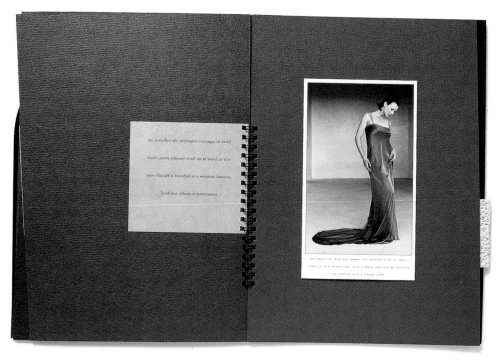

(this page left)
Design Firm: Michael Brock Design
Creative Director, Designer:
Michael Brock
Client: Warner Home Video

(this page right; opposite)
Design Firm: Gill Design
Art Director: Lisa Reynolds
Designer: Stephanie Conboy
Copywriter: Pattie Baker
Client: TNT

the new classics

WARNER HOME VIDEO INTRODUCES

the great movies of our time

YOU'LL NEVER FORGET WHEN YOU FIRST SAW THEM — IN A PACKED MOVIE THEATER, WHERE THE
EXCITEMENT OF A GREAT SHARED EXPERIENCE WAS MATCHED BY THE SENSE OF ANTICIPATION
AND THE THRILL OF AN EVENT. YOU REMEMBER THE TITLE SONG, THE CHARACTERS NAMES,
THE VERY BEST LINES. YOU HAVE A FAVORITE MOMENT. AND YOU ALWAYS — ALWAYS — WANT
TO SEE THESE MOVIES AGAIN, INSISTING THAT PEOPLE CLOSE TO YOU WATCH THEM, TOO,
IF THEY EVER HOPE TO TRULY UNDERSTAND YOU. THESE FILMS ARE THE NEW CLASSICS.

these movies define our lives

AND THEY NOW DEFINE TURNER NETWORK TELEVISION. WITH A ROUSING LINE-UP OF
NEW CLASSICS LIKE E.T., RAIN MAN, TOP GUN, THE SHAWSHANK REDEMPTION
AND SATURDAY NIGHT FEVER, TNT HAS BECOME A FAVORITE NETWORK OF TODAY'S
MOVIE AUDIENCES. AND THE HOME OF THE NEW CLASSICS.

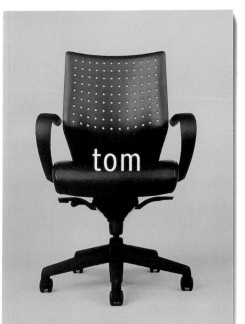

Design Firm: Concrete Design
Communications Inc.
Art Directors: John Pylypczak, Diti Katona
Designer, Copywriter: John Pylypczak
Photographer: Karen Levy
Client: Keilhauer

tom's

shy

it's midnight

already?

tom's on a

...roll

Design Firm: NB: Studio
Designers: Ben Stott, Nick Finney
Illustrator: Bump
Photographer: Steve Rees
Client: Knoll International

Design Firm: NB: Studio
Designers: Ben Stott, Nick Finney
Illustrator: Bump
Photographer: Steve Rees
Client: Knoll International

Homer

A key member of the PL1 product family is Homer a personal reference unit for the mobile workforce. Effectively a briefcase on wheels which can be pulled to a chosen worksetting. Homer provides two separate storage compartments. Behind a receding tambour door is space for personal effects and files, accessed from above is space for stationery items and a lap-top.

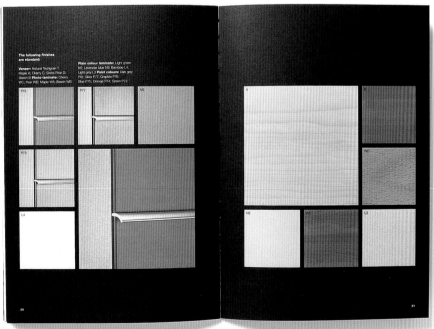

The following finishes are standard:

Veneer: Natural Techgrain T; Maple A; Cherry C; Swiss Pear D; Beech B **Photo-laminate:** Cherry WC; Pear WD; Maple WA; Beech WB

Plain colour laminate: Light green N5; Lavendar blue N9; Bamboo L4; Light grey L3 **Paint colours:** Dark grey P01; Silver P77; Graphite P76; Blue P75; Orange P74; Green P73

Design Firm: Liska & Associates
Creative Director: Steve Liska
Designer: Susan Carlson
Client: Heltzer Inc.

HELTZER incorporated

Design Firm: Werk 3 Graphic Design
Creative Director, Designer: Nicole Bryan
Client: Classicon GMB

Design Firm: Werk 3 Graphic Design
Creative Director, Designer: Nicole Bryan
Client: Classicon GMB

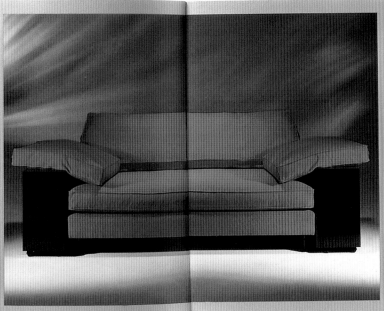

Kantige Kuben und weiche
Polster, Ästhetik und Kom-
fort: Eileen Gray's „Lota"
überwindet alle Wider-
sprüche und versöhnt alle
Dogmen.

Angular cubes and soft cus-
hions, aesthetics and com-
fort: Eileen Gray's "Lota"
surmounts all contradictions
and reconciles all dogma.

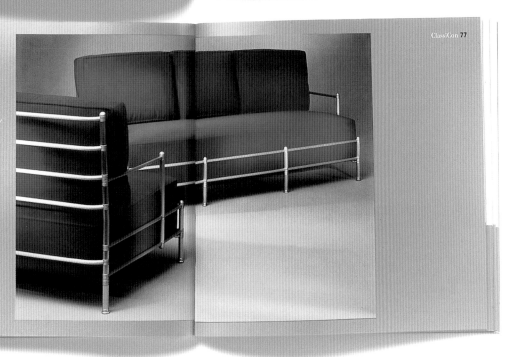

Warren McArthur's Sofa
„Ambassador" - wahrlich
ein Botschafter des zeitlos
guten Design.

Warren McArthur's sofa
"Ambassador" - truly a
representative of timelessly
good design.

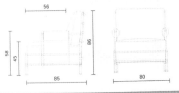 

AMBASSADOR

Gestell aus geschliffenem,
silber eloxiertem Aluminium.
Sitz aus Buchenrahmen mit
Gummigurten. Polsterung:
Polyurethan und Polyester-
watte. Loses Rückenkissen
aus Polyurethan und Dacron-
watte. Bezug aus Stoff oder
Leder.

45

76 x 76

Design Warren McArthur 1932

56

58   45   86

85   80

Frame of polished silver-
anodized aluminium.
Seat of beech wood frame
and rubber webbing.
Upholstery: polyurethane
and polyester filling. Loose
back pillow of polyurethane
and dacron filling. Cover in
fabric or leather.

Ob als Ergänzung zum „Ambassador"-Sofa oder als Solitär für Lesestunden in der
Bibliothek - der „Ambassador"-Sessel ist stets ein aufsehenerregender Eye-catcher und
dank der üppigen Polsterung eine komfortable Ruheinsel. Der quadratische Hocker ist
der ideale Partner dieses Sessels, macht aber auch als frei plaziertes Einzelobjekt eine
ausgezeichnete Figur.

Whether in addition to the "Ambassador"-sofa or alone for reading in the library the
"Ambassador"-armchair is always a sensational eye-catcher and thanks to the luxurios
upholstery also a comfortable place to rest. The square stool is the ideal partner for this
armchair, but even placed freely as a single object it has an excellent appearance.

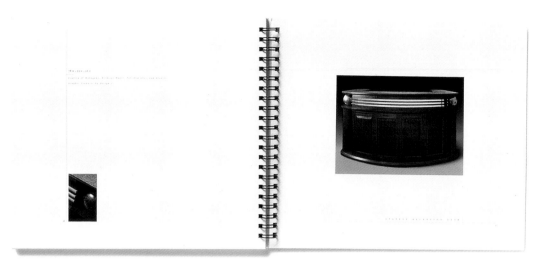

Design Firm: Basler Design Group
Designers: Bill Basler, Drew Davies
Copywriter: Bill Basler
Client: Schwartzkopf Fine Woodworking

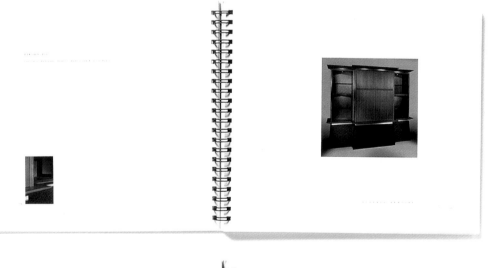

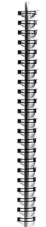

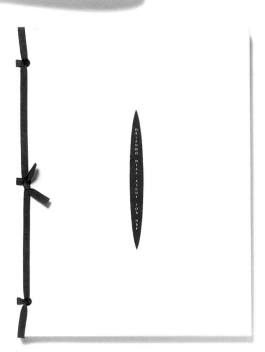

(this page; following spread)
Design Firm: Vanderbyl Design
Designer: Michael Vanderbyl
Photographer: Hedrich Blessing
Copywriter: Penny Benda
Client: Hickory Business Furniture

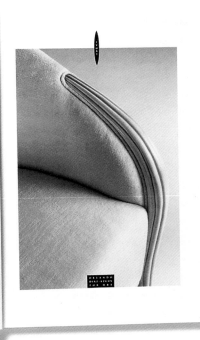

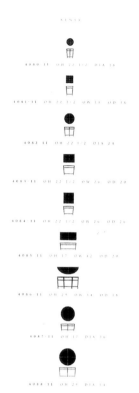

4080-11   OH 22 1/2   DIA 18

4081-11   OH 22 1/2   OW 15   OD 18

4082-11   OH 22 1/2   DIA 24

4083-11   OH 22 1/2   OW 26   OD 20

4084-11   OH 22 1/2   OW 26   OD 26

4085-11   OH 17   OW 42   OD 20

4086-11   OH 29   OW 34   OD 18

4087-11   OH 17   DIA 36

4088-11   OH 24   DIA 54

CHALICE

ORLANDO
DIAZ-AZCUY
FOR HBF

NUBIAN

7433-10   OH 37   OW 28 1/2   OD 45   AH 25 1/2

NUBIAN

7433-12   OH 35   OW 28 1/2   OD 45   AH 25 1/2

7434-10   OH 35   OW 60   OD 45   AH 25 1/2

7434-12   OH 35   OW 60   OD 45   AH 25 1/2

7435-10   OH 35   OW 75   OD 45   AH 25 1/2

7435-12   OH 35   OW 75   OD 45   AH 25 1/2

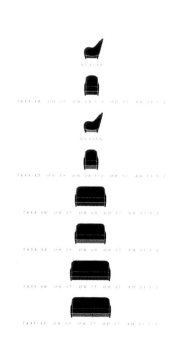

NUBIAN

ORLANDO
DIAZ-AZCUY
FOR HBF

IVORY

ORLANDO
DIAZ-AZCUY
FOR HBF

SONGHAI

ORLANDO
DIAZ-AZCUY
FOR HBF

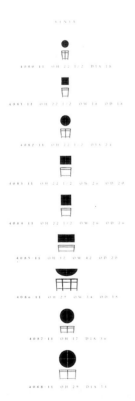

KENYA

4080-11   OH 22 1/2   DIA 18

4081-11   OH 22 1/2   OW 18   OD 18

4082-11   OH 22 1/2   DIA 24

4083-11   OH 22 1/2   OW 26   OD 20

4084-11   OH 22 1/2   OW 26   OD 26

4085-11   OH 17   OW 42   OD 20

4086-11   OH 29   OW 54   OD 19

4087-11   OH 17   DIA 36

4088-11   OH 29   DIA 54

KENYA

ORLANDO
DIAZ-AZCUY
FOR HBF

Winners
Lauréats

VIRTU 10 Canadian Design Competition: Work is submitted to the competition under two main categories: Home Furnishings or Consumer Products. Within these categories work then falls into three subgroups: In production, (prototype) intended for production, or limited edition

Concours de design canadien VIRTU 10 : Les soumissions au concours se classent dans deux grandes catégories : équipement ménager ou produits de consommation. Les objets sont ensuite répartis dans trois sous-groupes, soit en production, (prototype) prévu pour la production ou édition limitée.

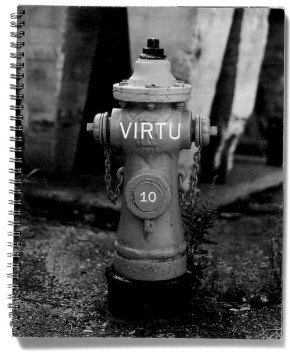

Design Firm: Concrete Design
Communications Inc.
Art Directors: Diti Katona, John Pylypczak
Designer: Nick Monteleone
Photographer: Ron Baxter Smith
Copywriter: Esther Shipman
Client: Virtu Mailbox 348

(opposite)
Design Firm: Knoll Graphics (in-house)
Art Directors, Designers: Chris Solwar,
Lucy Pope
Client: Knoll Graphics

ROBERT & TRIX HAUSSMANN · Haussmann Lounge Seating, KnollStudio, 1986
Metamorphosis, Study for a "Pseudo-Bauhaus" Gobelin

75 YEARS OF BAUHAUS DESIGN
1919 1994

JOHN RIZZI · Interaction Tables, 1991

t ink

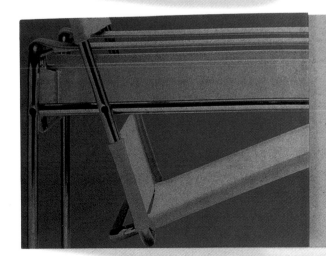

Knoll Celebrates 75 Years Of Bauhaus Design, 1919-1994

Design Firm: Michael Kaspar Visuelle
Communication
Art Director: Michael Kaspar
Photographer: Martin Wolf
Copywriter: Petra Jung
Client: Matthias Tenhaeff Holzindustrie
Hunsrück

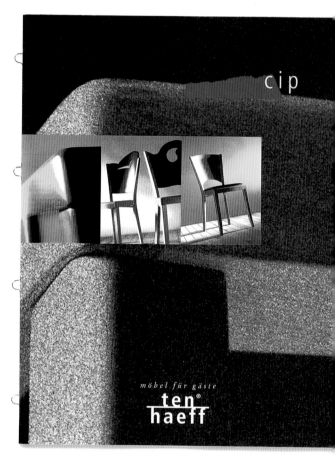

cip

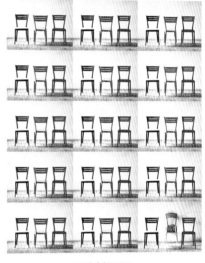

Stuhl 3692, Tisch 262 mit Holzsäule, Tisch 432 mit Metallsäule

Stuhl 3692, Tisch 262 mit Holzsäule, Tisch 434 mit Metallsäule

cip

Stuhl 3693

möbel für gäste

ten haeff®

Stuhl 3693

cip

Stühle 3686, 3693

möbel für gäste

ten haeff®

Stühle 3687, 3689, 3688

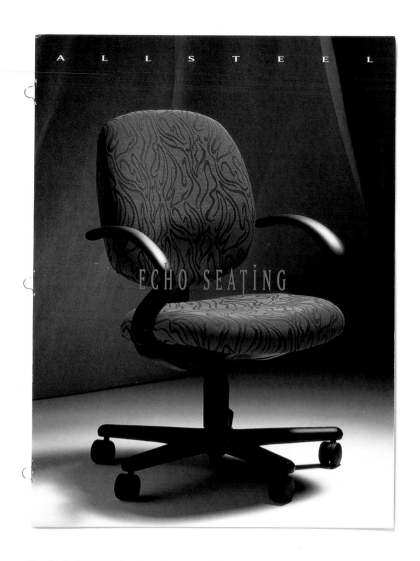

ECHO SEATING

ARIEL

Design Firm: GibbsBaronet
Creative Director, Designer: Steve Gibbs
Photographer: Andy Post
Copywriter: Gail Hannah
Client: Allsteel

In TOLLESON II, designers Tom Tolleson and Greg Saul have extended their highly successful chair line to include a task chair for people engaged in COMPUTER-INTENSIVE work. Tolleson II shares all the best Tolleson family traits: smoothly curved forms, beautifully rendered details and top-notch TAILORING. But Tolleson II has special characteristics designed to meet the needs of people who spend more than four hours a day at a keyboard and screen. It is smaller in SCALE, has a separate seat and back and includes a wider range of ERGONOMIC features targeted at relieving the shoulder strain, neck pain and repetitive stress injuries common to computer workers.

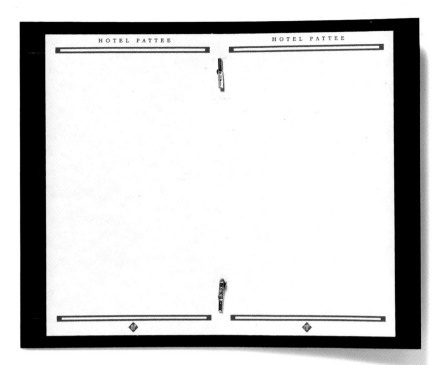

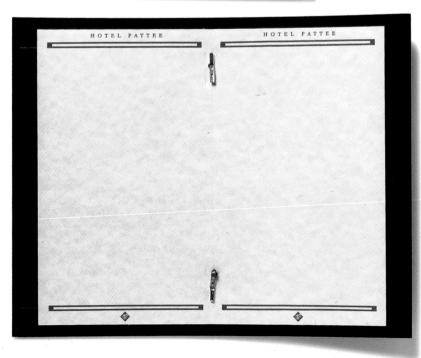

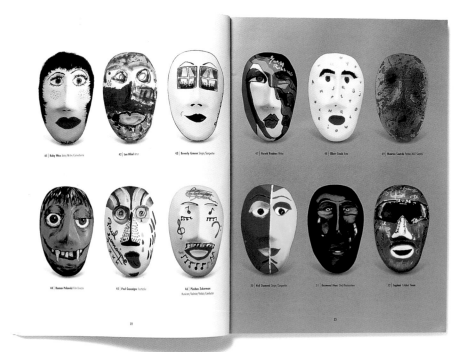

Design Firm: Hagari Design
Creative Director, Designer: Ilan Hagari
Client: Princes Trust Events Ltd.

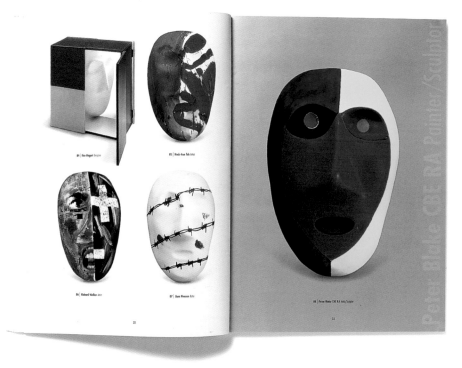

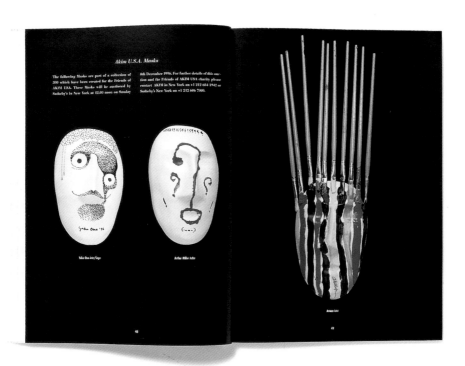

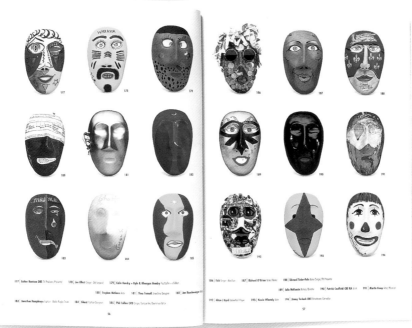

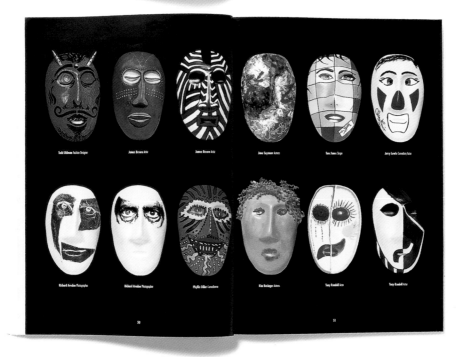

Design Firm: Marcus Lee Design
Creative Director: Marcus Lee
Designer: George Margaritis
Photographer: Rick Bawden
Client: Museum & Art Gallery
of the Northern Territory

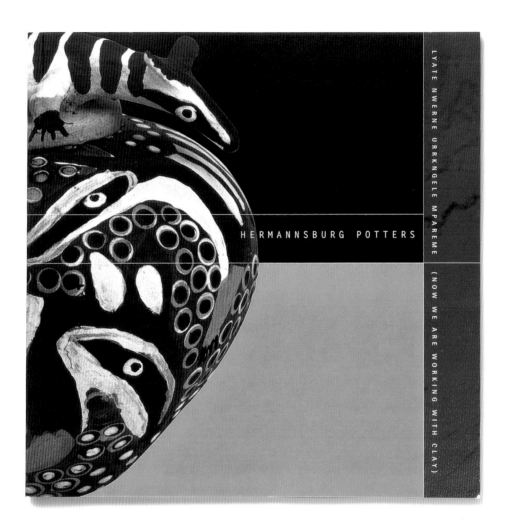

Esther Ngale Kennedy

Western Arrernte/Luritja language, domicile Hermannsburg (Ntaria), Marngpal Merne 1994, handcoiled terracotta, underglazes, glaze (interior), applied decoration, 28 x 20 cm. Collection of the Museum and Art Gallery of the Northern Territory, Darwin. (Aberb 3350)

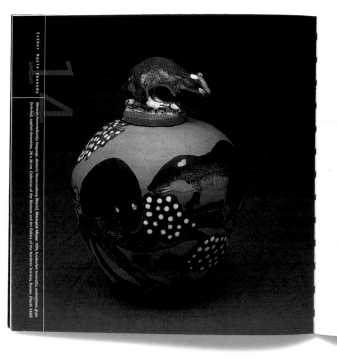

Dawn Ngale Wheeler

Western Arrernte/Luritja language, domicile Hermannsburg (Ntaria), Remeye (Lizards) 1994, handcoiled terracotta, underglazes, glaze (interior), applied decoration, 13 x 11 cm. Collection of the Museum and Art Gallery of the Northern Territory, Darwin. (Aberb 3340)

Arrernte language, domicile Hermannsburg (Ntaria), Irrpenge (Fish) 1993, handcoiled terracotta, underglazes, glaze (interior), 18 x 14.5 cm. Private Collection, Melbourne.

Kay Penangke Tucker

Kay Penangke Tucker

Western Arrernte language, domicile Hermannsburg (Ntaria), Ure (Fire) 1992, handcoiled terracotta, underglazes, glaze (interior), 13 x 13 cm. Collection of the Araluen Centre for Arts and Entertainment, Alice Springs.

Judith Pengarte Inkamala

Western Arrernte language, domicile Hermannsburg (Ntaria), Merry Christmas 1994, handcoiled terracotta, underglazes, glaze (interior), applied decoration, 16 x 9 cm. Private Collection, Alice Springs.

Noreen Ngale Hudson

Western Arrernte language, domicile Hermannsburg (Ntaria), Irretye Antywele Neme (Eagle Sitting on Nest) 1994, handcoiled terracotta, underglazes, glaze (interior), applied decoration, 23 x 16.5 cm. On loan from Alcaston House Gallery, Melbourne.

Judith Pengarte Inkamala

Western Arrernte language, domicile Hermannsburg (Ntaria), Irrwaltetye (Untitled) 1995, handcoiled terracotta, underglazes, glaze (interior), applied decoration, 24.5 x 23 cm. Collection of the Museum and Art Gallery of the Northern Territory, Darwin. (Aberb 3344). Acquisition assisted by the Australia Council.

Beryl Ngale Entata

Western Arrernte language, domicile Hermannsburg (Ntaria), Iretye (Pink Galahs) 1994, handcoiled terracotta, underglazes, glaze (interior), applied decoration, 30.5 x 19 cm. Collection of the Museum and Art Gallery of the Northern Territory, Darwin. (Aberb 3242). Acquisition assisted by the Australia Council.

Gwen Mpetyane Inkamala

Western Arrernte language, domicile Lyela Outstation, underglazes, glaze (interior), applied decoration, 12 x 14.5 cm. Collection of the Museum and Art Gallery of the Northern Territory, Darwin. (Aberb 3245). Acquisition from the Shell Aboriginal Art Fund.

Gwen Mpetyane Inkamala

Tyelpe (Quail) 1996, handcoiled terracotta.

Gwen Mpetyane Inkamala

Western Arrernte language, domicile Lyela Outstation, Rele (My People) 1994, handcoiled terracotta, underglazes, glaze (interior), applied decoration, 19.5 x 17 cm. Private Collection, Melbourne.

Design Firm: Publications & Graphics
Brigham Young University
Creative Director, Designer:
Rebecca Sterrett
Copywriter: Herman DuToit
Client: Brigham Young University
Museum of Art

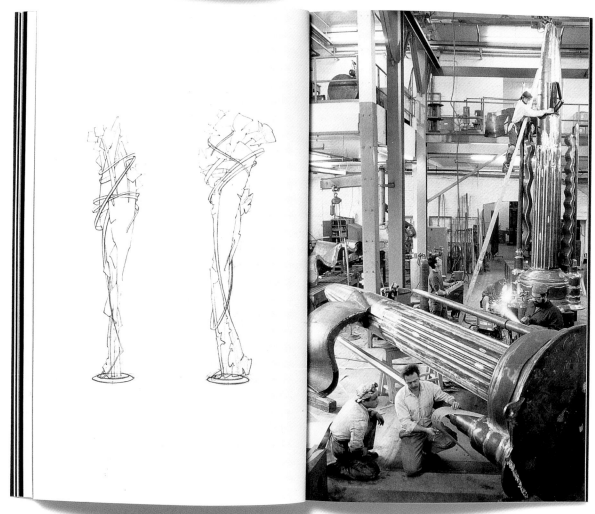

Photographer, painter and video artist William Wegman, with his Weimaraner pets Man Ray, Fay Ray and Battina, has made a career of inventing and documenting the antics of his dogs. In 1970 when Wegman bought his first dog, Man Ray, as a pet, he had no idea that the pup would wander into his photo shoots and insist on being "part of the action." At some point, it became easier for the photographer to incorporate the dog into his work than to lure him out.

The black and white early 1970s images of Man Ray changed by the end of the decade to the brilliantly colored grainless images produced by a new Polaroid 20"x 24" camera. It is these Polaroids of more recent pets, Fay Ray and Battie, from Wegman's personal collection that are the first creatures of **Wildlife**. • In the 1970s Wegman began to dress Man Ray in costumes. With these outfits, and later with elaborate sets, the dog began to assume human behaviors: in bed watching TV, wearing nail polish, and in a canoe in Indian headdress. • In a continual parade of images from elegant abstractions with the dog posed on cubes to familiar narratives like the fairy tales **Cinderella** and **Little Red Riding Hood**, Wegman's dogs are human surrogates. Their doleful gaze as they participate in the rituals of our species—marriage ceremonies, housekeeping, and preening in front of a mirror—inspire both humor and self reflection. Somehow two dogs lying in bed together, their paws draped over the fold of the covers intently watching TV, makes a stronger statement about our culture than people depicted in the same pose ever could. • Wegman lets the dogs play themselves and thus selects them for roles based on their own personalities. The artist thinks that dogs are the only animals that care about people, and is painfully aware that he will experience the loss of six generations of caring dogs in his lifetime. He watches and documents as the puppy becomes the adolescent, then all too quickly reaches maturity and progresses to old age. • After 23 years of working with dogs, Wegman's collaboration with his animals is such that he can conspire with them to imitate a sweet grandmother or a vicious wolf. Recent book projects include **ABC** and **1,2,3** in which the dogs' bodies are arranged to form letters and numbers. • The dogs will assume super sleuth poses in **The Hardly Boys**, a spoof on the boys' mystery series of the 1940s. • Fay Ray and Battie come to their master and ask him to play with them. Since their master is Wegman, the "playing" becomes art.

The artistic life of sculptor Dennis Oppenheim is marked by variety. His pioneering projects in the 1960s and 1970s include performance and conceptual works as well as process pieces that investigate his own body and the landscape. If any thread can be found in the disparate forms of Oppenheim's oeuvre it is his feverish search for the roots of transformation—alchemical formulas that make lightning strike, teeth chatter, and send the stuff of this world flying into the air. The six deer that circle the gallery to form 1993's **Digestion: Gypsum Gypsies** began as a single animal. For the artist the antlers of the deer seemed to want to become a candelabra—yet this alteration did not suggest a familiar species, but one the artist invents to explore ideas of time, mutation, and metaphysical power. • In another permutation of **Digestion**, the four flaming deer were bisected and attached to the walls of the gallery—seeming to appear and disappear through the plasterboard. The artist thought of the animals as "gypsum gypsies" that were both digesting the wall and drawing energy from it. The flaming horns suggest that the bodies of the animals are furnaces that can "breathe fire" like a dragon. This alchemical transformation adds a performance component to the static form and allows the animals to become an armature for Oppenheim's ideas about the violence of change, the vacillation between life and death, abstraction, real time, and the deep-rooted psychological states suggested by heat and danger. • In this most recent (1992) permutation of **Digestion**, the six deer are no longer attached to the wall but circle the gallery and confront each other. Several seem to paw the ground with heads down as they tilt their fiery antlers. • A lineage can be traced back to Oppenheim's work with live animals in the 1970s (a parrot, a dog, a tarantula), but this recent **Digestion** is less transactional and more removed from real time. It exemplifies the artist's need to continually find a blank slate and create a mystique that challenges life's mysteries rather than establishing a signature style. It is in this quest for magic that Oppenheim finds the psychic strength to threaten his art-historical position, face life's challenges, and create action-oriented works that throb.

Design Firm: Mires Design
Art Director: John Ball
Designers: John Ball, Gail Spitzley
Copywriter: Reese Shaw
Client: California Center for the Arts

WILLIAM WEGMAN
INNUENDO CHAIR 1992
POLAROID
24 x 20 INCHES

DONALD ROLLER WILSON
COOKIE WANTED IT—(MISS TEXAS—
THE CROWN)—BUT, MEG GOT IT—(MISS
TEXAS—THE CROWN), 1992/93
OIL ON TWO PANELS
51 7/8 X 9 3/4 INCHES EACH

WILDLIFE BY JEFF KELLY

When I was in high school only girls drew horses. I drew the skull of a steer, taking four months to account for its every weathered crack and bony flake. It was dry and minimal, like the desert landscape of southern Nevada where I lived. It had metaphorical distance—it was cool—because of its deadness. While the skull was drawn in the style of Andrew Wyeth, its sensibility was of the inert, industrial and natural materials then being used by minimalist sculptors and land artists of whom I was only vaguely aware. (Later, in art school, Robert Smithson would become my hero.) Horses were girl art. • Looking back, my anti-horse bias was indicative of broader cultural biases about the proper subject matter of art at the time. As a young artist, my sense of nature was of its esthetic abstractions: of its space, time, process, materiality, light, and so on. It was an empirical resource for artists. "Nature" in its more figural incarnations—like animals—was thought to be sentimental, unworthy of serious artistic activity. The romanticism it evoked was to be avoided at all costs. One result was that while I steered clear of horses I also subordinated all other wildlife in my unconscious hierarchy of esthetic subject matter. Our subjects—"space," "surface," "color," "paint"—had to be like our objects, and while this reduction of terms was among the particular contributions of Minimalism to American art, it nonetheless tended to limit the range of permissible subjects for artists. Like the human figure in painting and sculpture around 1970, animals were out of style. • Then I saw my first Deborah Butterfield horses. Composed of twisted, corrugated tin or woven of sticks and mud, they were among the most poetic things I'd ever seen. They seemed suspended between esthetic categories: were they sculptures, drawings in space, or, when in groups of two or three, installations (herds)? Because of this ambiguity, as well as their real life scale, they fell back upon some essential identification with their subject matter—horses. You didn't have to squint at the "art" to see its meaning or feel its presence. Some quality of horseness was held inside them like a spirit. It was so palpable that you hesitated to get too close, half-wondering if the things would move. • Like debris washed up along the edge of a creek after the flood waters recede, Butterfield's horses have a residual presence. They represent what's left after the artist's encounter with the landscape where she finds the parts that will compose them. All their sticks and straw and scrap metal seem held in a

his turkeys are what Jim Lewis calls "antitotems," the purpose of which is to deny the sense of cultural and psychological place—one's sense of identity—that totems (and other cultural fetishes) are meant to foster. These are not about animals, or even systems of animal classification. They are semiotic turkeys, parodies of cultural identity, and might be understood as a critique of multiculturalism as a "postmodern" form of tribal classification. As Lewis puts it, "there are no natural kinds." • Well, I'm not so sure. I think what this show suggests is that there are countless natural kinds, and that it continues to be a mistake to believe that we are not among them. Sure, cultural identity is a slippery issue these days, but that does not automatically make turkeys into human signifiers. The larger question is not whether we—animals all—are natural, but whether naturalness is a human-centered value that no longer applies. When used as a term that justifies unchecked human "progress" in the eco-sphere, nature, a purely cultural ideal, is just another form of global violence. It remains crucial that we stop seeing nature and culture as opposites in a dialectical pair, for the dialogue between them has proven to be an unbalanced monologue—a rhetoric of human dominion over the earth. • Rather, it is the interdependence of culture and nature that most of the artists in **Wildlife** seem to be thinking about in their various depictions of animals. This kind of thinking is also a feature of what has lately been termed "eco-feminism," and reminds me once again of my adolescent estimations of "girl art." In retrospect, it was the girls more than the boys of

my generation who made the greatest impact upon the arts. With feminism, a new wave of human "nature," which understood its connection to culture and politics, was unleashed. Its energies—sometimes destructive, sometimes preservational—opened up closed systems of thought and action, much as the Wild Animal Park of Escondido—and places like it—helped open up Victorian ideas of "the zoo." In this opening up, our relationships with nature and its "other" citizens have slowly begun to change. • Expressed in those changing relationships are some of the most compelling and significant ethical and environmental dilemmas of the late twentieth century, contests for rights and resources that foreshadow those of the century to come. The questions of animal life, consciousness, and habitat are central to our changing perspectives of ourselves as members, but not rulers, of the planet. Moving from an ego-centered, anthropocentric stance against nature that reflects our limited understanding of the universe, we have begun in the last two decades to see ourselves as one species intertwined among others in a brilliantly complex ecosystem of interdependencies. To know that the world beyond us—and perhaps within us—is more complicated than we can think is also to imagine—indeed, to submit to—a future in which humans are no longer at the center of things. At the same time, it opens up in the human center a meeting place for all things great and small.
Jeff Kelley (Art critic and visiting lecturer at the University of California, Berkeley) for Naomi

ALEXIS ROCKMAN
EVOLUTION (DETAIL), 1992

RICHARD SHAFER
JERUSALEM CRICKET, 1992; HORSE LUBBER GRASSHOPPER, 1992;
PAINTED GRASSHOPPER, 1992; EASTERN WOOD TICK, 1992;
KEELED SHIELD-BACK KATYDID, 1992; MARBLED DIVING BEETLE, 1992;
ELEPHANT STAG BEETLE, 1992; STREAK WINGED RED SKIMMER, 1992;
BLUE MANTIDFLY, 1992
OIL ON BOARD
24 X 24 INCHES EACH

RENEE PETROPOULOS
NORTHERN EUROPEAN GAME, FISH AND FOWL, 1992
OIL ON PANEL
48 INCHES IN DIAMETER

*I*magine diving into the waters of the outer bay, suspended in the open water far from the shore and far above the seafloor. There's no seaweed for shelter here, no rocky reefs to rest upon; endless blue water surrounds you. There's a world of life here, a world alive. Much of it drifts by without your even seeing it: a multitude of plankton too tiny, too transparent, to see. Yet other life looms large. Schools of streamlined mackerel and bonito speed past. Seven-foot ocean sunfish flap by. Yellowfin tuna, quintessential ocean swimmers, power their way through the water. Green sea turtles,

10

visitors from the tropics, cruise lazily. The Outer Bay exhibit–the stunning one-million gallon centerpiece of the new wing–carries you to the very heart of the outer bay. Gazing into its blue depths through the largest aquarium window in the world, you feel as if you're looking into the far ocean reaches. Stand and watch as schools of sleek silvery fishes flash by, turn as one and fade into the distance. Stand and picture a world of life, both large and small. Stand and imagine yourself suspended in the middle of open water sixty miles offshore.

11

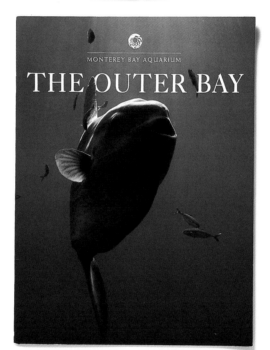

MONTEREY BAY AQUARIUM

THE OUTER BAY

Design Firm: Pentagram Design
Creative Director: Kit Hinrichs
Designer: Belle How
Copywriter: Michael Rigsby
Client: Monterey Bay Aquarium

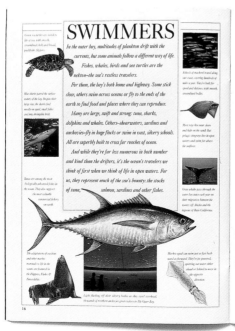

SWIMMERS

In the outer bay, multitudes of plankton drift with the currents, but some animals follow a different way of life. Fishes, whales, birds and sea turtles are the nekton–the sea's restless travelers.

For them, the bay's both home and highway. Some stick close, others swim across oceans or fly to the ends of the earth to find food and places where they can reproduce.

Many are large, swift and strong: tuna, sharks, dolphins and whales. Others–shearwaters, sardines and anchovies–fly in huge flocks or swim in vast, silvery schools. All are superbly built to cross far reaches of ocean.

And while they're far less numerous in both number and kind than the drifters, it's the ocean's travelers we think of first when we think of life in open waters. For us, they represent much of the sea's bounty: the stocks of tuna, salmon, sardines and other fishes.

16

17

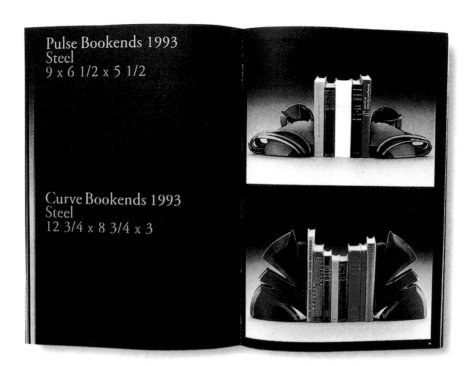

Pulse Bookends 1993
Steel
9 x 6 1/2 x 5 1/2

Curve Bookends 1993
Steel
12 3/4 x 8 3/4 x 3

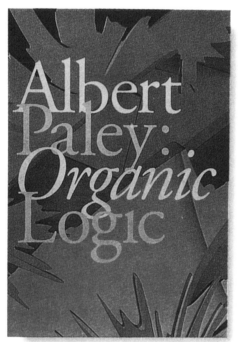

Design Firm: Pentagram Design
Art Director: Michael Bierut
Designer: Esther Bridavsky
Photographer: Bruce Miller
Client: Peter Joseph Gallery

Zig Zag 1994
Steel, mahogany,
stainless steel
30 x 84 x 24

(this spread; following page)
Design Firm: Mires Design
Art Director: Scott Mires
Deigners: Scott Mires, Miguel Perez
Photographer: Chris Wimpey
Client: Taylor Guitars

(this spread; following page)
Design Firm: Mires Design
Art Director: Scott Mires
Deigners: Scott Mires, Miguel Perez
Photographer: Chris Wimpey
Client: Taylor Guitars

900 series

The 900 Series is distinctive for its gorgeous inlay, yet the tonal properties create an even more dramatic impression. This rich sound comes from master-grade Engelmann sound-boards, coupled with the highest quality Indian rosewood. Accents include wood binding throughout, and tops bordered with a colorful band of abalone. These exquisite instruments set a new standard among rosewood guitars, in both tone and appearance. Regardless of which model you choose, a 900 Series guitar certainly will inspire you to play your best. It's the embodiment of beauty and musical inspiration.

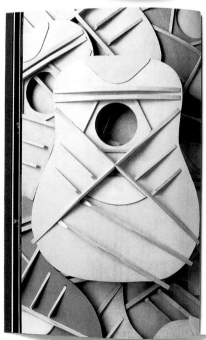

600 series

Curly maple is perhaps the most visually exciting wood found on guitars. We use stains and a gloss finish to accentuate its dramatic figure, and we complement the wood with deluxe binding and inlay. Maple Taylors are favorites with guitarists who amplify their acoustic sound. Controlled overtones and even response from the lowest to the highest notes provide an ideal signal source for the Fishman dual-source pickup system. It's the perfect recipe for a contemporary stage guitar. The 600 Series now comes in a natural finish, or in stunning transparent colors — amber, red, black, blue, or green.

300 series

In recent years, the original 300 Series grew to include several ironwoods. Now, the mahogany versions get their own series number. The idea of no-frills value remains unchanged. 300 Series features include solid-wood construction, an ebony fretboard and pin bridge, Grover tuners, and scalloped top bracing. There are no unbound body edges, no laminates, and the finish on the top is buffed to a high gloss. Cutaway models include a Fishman pickup with onboard electronics. Despite the easy-friendly price tag, the tone and playability found on every 300 Series guitar is pure Taylor.

"Now, I can get pretty excited about good guitars, but generally I get over it in five minutes. But this guitar just makes me play it. It just sounds so good. A pretty amazing guitar. Over the years, I'd heard a few vintage guitars that had a real bright, sparkly, bell-like tone that impressed me, and I decided to build a new guitar to produce that sound."

BOB TAYLOR, ON DESIGNING THE GRAND AUDITORIUM GUITAR.

1995 LIMITED EDITION SERIES

MODEL
GA-MC
TOP
Western Red Cedar
BACK/SIDES
Tropical Mahogany

BINDING
Tortoiseshell
INLAY
1995 GA Pattern
QUANTITY
300

TAYLOR GUITARS

Taylor Guitars
1995 LIMITED EDITION SERIES

1995 LIMITED EDITION SERIES

MODEL
GA-KC
TOP
Western Red Cedar
BACK/SIDES
Hawaiian Koa

BINDING
Rosewood/Abalone
INLAY
1995 GA Pattern
QUANTITY
100

TAYLOR GUITARS

1995 LIMITED EDITION SERIES

MODEL
GA-RS
TOP
Sitka Spruce
BACK/SIDES
Hawaiian Koa

BINDING
Rosewood/Abalone
INLAY
1995 GA Pattern
QUANTITY
100

TAYLOR GUITARS

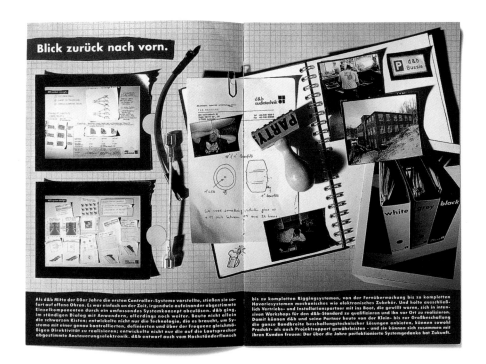

Blick zurück nach vorn.

Als d&b Mitte der 80er Jahre die ersten Controller-Systeme vorstellte, stießen sie sofort auf offene Ohren. Es war einfach an der Zeit, irgendwie aufeinander abgestimmte Einzelkomponenten durch ein umfassendes Systemkonzept abzulösen. d&b ging, im ständigen Dialog mit Anwendern, allerdings noch weiter. Baute nicht allein die schwarzen Kisten; entwickelte nicht nur die Technologie, die es braucht, um Systeme mit einer genau kontrollierten, definierten und über der Frequenz gleichmäßigen Direktivität zu realisieren; entwickelte nicht nur die auf die Lautsprecher abgestimmte Ansteuerungselektronik. d&b entwarf auch vom Hochständerflansch

bis zu kompletten Riggingsystemen, von der Fernüberwachung bis zu kompletten Havariesystemen mechanisches wie elektronisches Zubehör. Und holte ausschließlich Vertriebs- und Installationspartner mit ins Boot, die gewillt waren, sich in intensiven Workshops für den d&b-Standard zu qualifizieren und ihn vor Ort zu realisieren. Damit können d&b und seine Partner heute von der Klein- bis zur Großbeschallung die ganze Bandbreite beschallungstechnischer Lösungen anbieten, können sowohl Produkt- als auch Projektsupport gewährleisten - und sie können sich zusammen mit ihren Kunden freuen: Der über die Jahre perfektionierte Systemgedanke hat Zukunft.

Design Firm: SWF & F Büros
für Werbung
Creative Director, Designer:
Barbara Waibel
Photographer: Helmut Ehmann
Copywriter: Uwe Schneider
Client: D & B Autotechnik

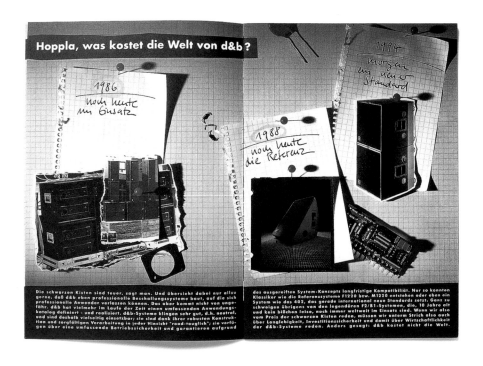

Hoppla, was kostet die Welt von d&b?

Die schwarzen Kisten sind teuer, sagt man. Und übersieht dabei nur allzu gerne, daß d&b eben professionelle Beschallungssysteme baut, auf die sich professionelle Anwender verlassen können. Das aber kommt nicht von ungefähr, d&b hat vielmehr im Laufe der Zeit einen umfassenden Anwendungskatalog definiert - und damit realisiert. d&b-Systeme klingen sehr gut, d.h. neutral, und sind deshalb vielseitig einsetzbar; sie sind dank ihrer robusten Konstruktion und sorgfältigen Verarbeitung in jeder Hinsicht "road-tauglich"; sie verfügen über eine umfassende Betriebssicherheit und garantieren aufgrund

des ausgereiften System-Konzepts langfristige Kompatibilität. Nur so konnten Klassiker wie die Referenzsysteme F1220 bzw. M1220 entstehen oder eben ein System wie das 402, das gerade international neue Standards setzt. Ganz zu schweigen übrigens von den legendären F2/F81-Systemen, die 10 Jahre alt und kein bißchen leise, noch immer weltweit im Einsatz sind. Wenn wir also vom Preis der schwarzen Kisten reden, müssen wir unterm Strich also auch über Langlebigkeit, Investitionssicherheit und damit über Wirtschaftlichkeit der d&b-Systeme reden. Anders gesagt: d&b kostet nicht die Welt.

FREEMAN
LAU 劉小康訊
WORKS 息的
OF 存在与再現
MESSAGE

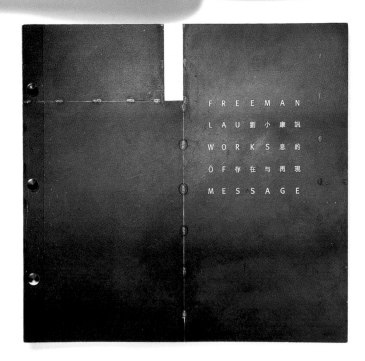

Design Firm: Kan & Lau
Design Consultants
Creative Director,
Art Director: Kan Tai Keung
Designers: Kan Tai Keung,
Benjamin Wongwai
Client: Kan & Lau
Design Consultants

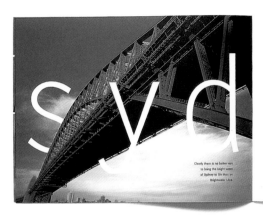

Clearly there is no better way to bring the bright water of Sydney to life than an Brightwater Ultra

Australians from China, Italy, Greece and Vietnam brought their appetites for fishy feasts to a city well-endowed with succulent sea-creatures. Even the evil food empire

of Britain has contributed. Fish and chips has been transformed ... ally by a Greek gentleman called Stiveca = into a yummy sit-down snack

fishy fare

Brightwater Ultra in *Sydney*

Design Firm: FGI
Creative Director, Art Director,
Designer, Copywriter: Nick Law
Photographer: Sean Izzard
Client: Crown Vantage

Every Sydney beach has a swimming pool, replenished by the tide. These pools are perfect for wave-shy tourists from landlocked countries who would rather swallow still water than get sand in their ears. But they weren't built for visiting Slovaks and Mongolians, they were built for bleary-eyed locals who make the pilgrimage every morning. Members of this strange aquatic cult span the generations, from water wings to blue rinse bathing caps. The older, the more devout. Can you imagine how many laps an 80 year old has swum? Is the bottom of a pool really that interesting? For Sydneysiders, swimming laps must be in the gene pool.

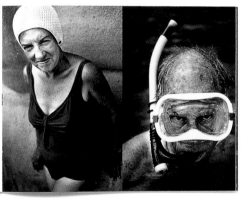

A few miles off the Sydney shore there is a net which keeps the finned foe at bay. So most folk have no fear of sharks. In fact Sydneysiders are quite fond of them. Batter-fried, with chips. A common sight, man eating shark.

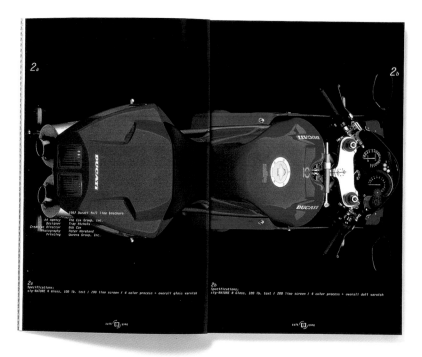

Design Firm: Douglas Oliver Design Office
Creative Director, Art Director, Designer:
Deanna Kuhlmann Leavitt
Client: Mead Coated Papers

No pun intended, but THIRST finds Signature to be a JOY to print! The Chicago Board of Trade Annual Report just won Best Printed in the 1997 AR100 show. Now, that says a lot about its performance. Of course, we selected Signature for the THIRST portfolio for all the right reasons. Its next performance will be the Lyric Opera of Chicago's 1998 Amistad Poster."

Barbara Valicenti, THIRST

THIRST
Self-Promotion

Design   THIRST
Creative Director   Rick Valicenti
Illustration   Mauro King
Printing   MPR Printing

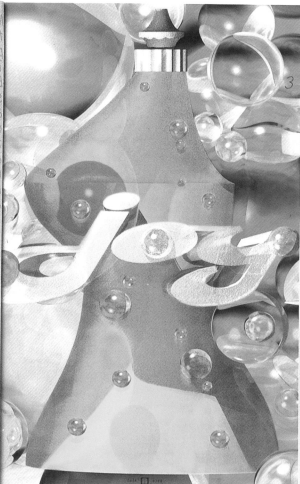

How's that for an encore?

Some things are worth repeating... like the great work that's been printed on Signature during the past year.

Mead Coated Papers would like to thank everyone who participated in our promotion. Without you, Signature never would have become a preferred Number One sheet.

Talk to us. Fill out the accompanying business reply card or call 1.800.345.6323 x 53308. Tell us what you think...about Signature, this promotion, other coated papers from Mead.

Specifications:
sig-NATURE R Dull, 100 lb. text / black + process undercolor + overall dull varnish

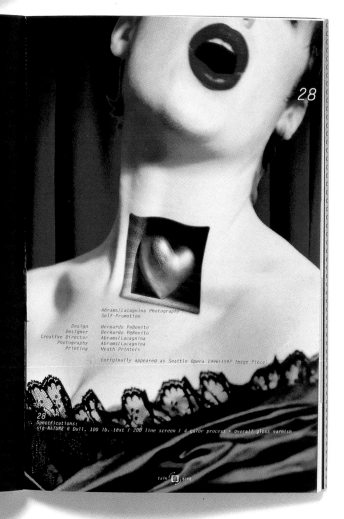

Abrams/Lacagnina Photography
Self-Promotion

Design   Bernardo PeBenito
Designer   Bernardo PeBenito
Creative Director   Abrams/Lacagnina
Photography   Abrams/Lacagnina
Printing   Heath Printers

(originally appeared as Seattle Opera 1996/1997 Image Piece)

28
Specifications:
sig-NATURE R Dull, 100 lb. text / 200 line screen / 4 color process + overall gloss varnish

FISH

CAKE

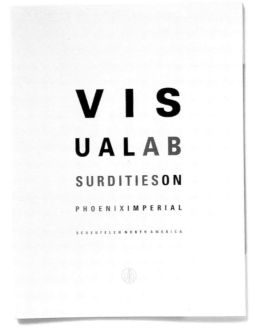

VIS
UALAB
SURDITIESON

PHOENIXIMPERIAL

SCHEUFELEN NORTH AMERICA

Design Firm:
Brian J. Ganton & Associates
Creative Director, Copywriter:
Brian J. Ganton
Art Director: Mark E. Ganton
Photographer: Christopher J. Ganton
Client: Scheufelen North America

TYPE

With that face, you'll be typecast.

YOU'RE NOT MY TYPE. BUT WHAT A FACE.

WHAT A FACE, YOU'RE JUST MY TYPE.

You know the type. You see their faces everywhere.

That type could always put a smile on her face.

FACE

SKY SCRAPER

FAN

Buzz down the highway on a ninety degree day and appreciate your lovely fan belt. Yeah, it cools your radiator.

BELT

Design Firm: MH' Éditions
Art Director, Designer: Michel Hosszu
Client: RMN: Réunion des Musées Nationaux

ADVENTURE HAS
ITS PLACE.
IN THE MOVIES.
IN THEME PARKS.
BUT IN THE
WORKPLACE, WE
WANT NO SURPRISES.
WE WANT A TOOL
WE CAN COUNT ON.
LIKE THIS.
AS BRIGHT AND
CONSTANT AS THE
NORTHERN STAR.

IN ATHLETICS,
THERE CAN
BE NO LIES. YOU
SAY YOU CAN RUN
THE FORTY IN 4.4?
WELL, HERE'S FORTY
YARDS. HERE'S
A STOP WATCH.
YOU'VE EITHER GOT
IT, OR YOU DON'T.
WE'VE GOT IT.
RIGHT HERE.
THERE CAN BE NO
DOUBT.

THIS IS AN AGE
OF EXPERTISE.
A SPECIALIST
DOES ONLY ONE
THING WELL.
BUT SOMETIMES
YOU MUST REACH
FOR A WORKHORSE.
A MULTI-TALENTED,
EASILY-ADAPTABLE,
DO-IT-ALL ALLY.
HERE IT IS
RIGHT AT HAND.
REACH FOR IT.

Design Firm:
Pentagram Design, Inc.
Creative Director,
Art Director:
Kit Hinrichs
Designer:
Amy Chan
Photographers:
Bob Esparza,
Brian Mahany
Illustrators:
Milton Glaser,
Barbara Banthien,
Seymour Chwast
Copywriter:
Delphine Hirasuna
Client: Simpson/
Fox River
Paper Company

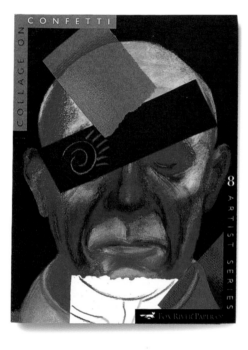

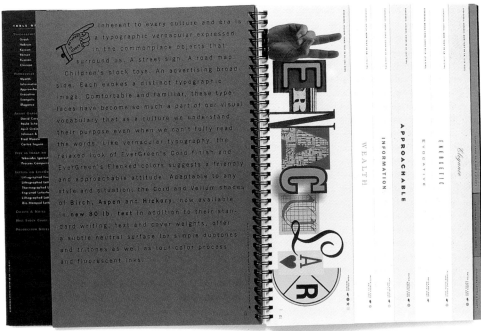

Design Firm: Pollard Design
Photographers: Jim Coon, Stan Waldhauser
Client: Strathmore Papers

Illustrators: Maira Kalman,
Mats Gustafson
Client: Strathmore Papers

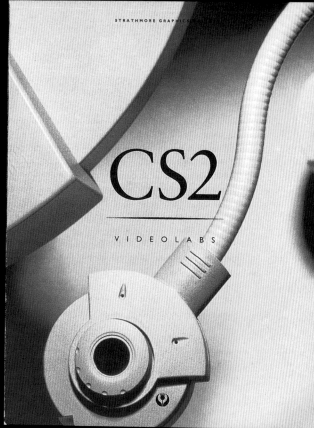

(opposite)
Design Firm: Designframe
Creative Director: James A. Sebastian
Art Director: Michael McGinn
Designers: Sharon Gresh,
Alexander Polakov
Photographers: Jim Cooper,
Craig Cutler, Nola Lopez,
James Sebastian, James Wojcik
Illustrators: Maira Kalman,
Mats Gustafson
Client: Strathmore Papers

19102030405060700

STRATHMORE WRITING COVER · BRIGHT WHITE · WOVE · COVER 80

STRATHMORE ELEMENTS · BRIGHT WHITE · SPIRAL · TEXT 80

IN THE 1990s, AT THE END OF THE MILLENNIUM, A CULTURE SEARCHES FOR ITS INNER CHILD—AND FINDS IT IN THE BRIGHT, ARTIFICIAL TONES OF THE INTERNET, TELEVISION, AND, ESPECIALLY, OUR TOOL, THE NINETIES HAS BEEN A RETRO DECADE, A TIME OF STUDIED RECAPITULATION. FIFTIES PASTELS, SIXTIES PSYCHEDELIA, AND SEVENTIES EARTH TONES HAVE REAPPEARED, BUT IN SLIGHTLY AMENDED FORM, AS DESIGNERS "SAMPLE" DECADES USING NEW TECHNOLOGIES. AMERICANS SEEM MORE WILLING TO EXPERIMENT WITH COLOR THAN EVER BEFORE. THE BABY BOOMERS, RETLIE AND AFFLUENT, CONFIDENT IN THEIR DESIGN DECISIONS, NEED VIBRANT COLORS TO STIMULATE THE FADING VISION THAT ACCOMPANIES AGE. THE YOUNG ALSO HAVE MORE SPENDING POWER THAN AT ANY TIME, AND MANUFACTURERS HAVE USED FLUORESCENT AND CITRUS COLORS TO CATCH THEIR EYES. IN THE FUTURE, ARCHAEOLOGISTS WON'T HAVE TO DIG AROUND FOR POTTERY SHARDS; THEY CAN JUST DOWNLOAD OUR MAIL ORDER CATALOGS AND LEARN EVERYTHING THEY NEED TO KNOW ABOUT OUR COLORS—AND OUR VALUES.

marketable aspects of color

STRATHMORE TEXT + COVER

THE MOST INTERESTING THING ABOUT COLOR THESE DAYS IS
HOW IT APPEARS SIMULTANEOUSLY IN DIFFERENT APPLICATIONS.
MARY BETH MOORE, COLOR CONSULTANT

Design Firm: Tolleson Design
Art Director, Designer: Steve Tolleson
Photographer: John Casado
Copywriter: Lindsay Beaman
Client: Fox River Paper Company

VISUAL'S INTENDED AND ITS ABILITY TO PORTRAY A CLEAR AND FOCAL PERFORMANCE — A CONCISE, VISUAL MEANS TO SIMPLIFY COMPLEX INFORMATION, CLARIFY POINT-TO-YEAR COMPARISONS, AND OTHERWISE CHECK OFF FINANCIAL AND STATISTICAL DATA. FOR INSTANCE, A CREATIVE USE OF BAR CHARTS IN THE FINANCIAL HIGHLIGHTS PROVIDES A CLEAR SNAPSHOT OF THE WEB NUMBERS, OR ICONOGRAPHIC ELEMENTS RELATED TO THE COMPANY'S BUSINESS CAN STRENGTHEN THESE. IN A CHART, AT MAKE ITS CONTENTS EASIER TO DIGEST.

When it comes to presenting performance charts, the Confetti line of papers provides a strong foundation that enhances any graphic message without taking it over. Using Confetti means you have the technical performance to design as straightforwardly or intricately as you desire. Which leads us to the question: how do we chart our own design performance, especially given the qualitative nature of our industry? The answer of course is: informed opinion, through a peer review in any number of judged shows. To keep the main design shows and their entry dates in mind, herewith are their names and contact information. See you by the punch bowl.

2

CLIENT
GROWTH

PRINT
104 Fifth Avenue
N.Y. N.Y. 10011
212 · 463 · 0600
DEADLINE / MARCH 15

THE 100 SHOW
American Center For Design
233 East Ontario Suite 500
Chicago, Illinois 60611
312 · 787 · 2018
DEADLINE / MAY

TYPE DIRECTORS SHOW
60 East 42nd Street Suite 1511
N.Y. N.Y. 10165 10165
212 · 983 · 6042
DEADLINE / JANUARY

11

ART DIRECTORS CLUB OF LOS ANGELES
5000 Hollywood Blvd. Suite 674
L.A. CA. 90028
213 · 465 · 1501
DEADLINE / OCTOBER

AR 100
866 3rd Avenue 24th floor
N.Y. N.Y. 10022
212 · 264 · 1880
DEADLINE / APRIL

AIGA GRAPHIC DESIGN U.S.A.
1059 3rd Avenue
N.Y. N.Y. 10021
212 · 752 · 0813
DEADLINE / JANUARY

GROWTH

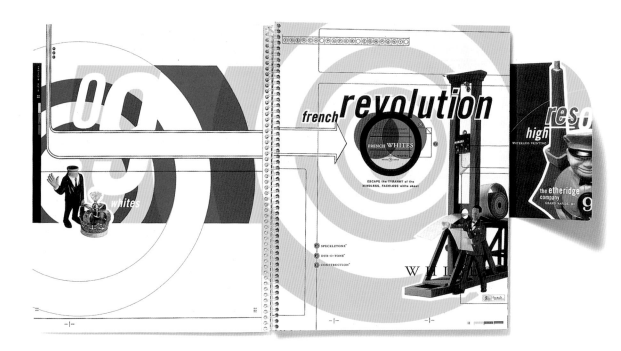

Design Firm: Charles S. Anderson
Design Company
Art Director: Charles S. Anderson
Designer: Jason Schulte
Photographer: Plastock/CSA Archive
Copywriter: Lisa Pemrick
Client: French Paper Company

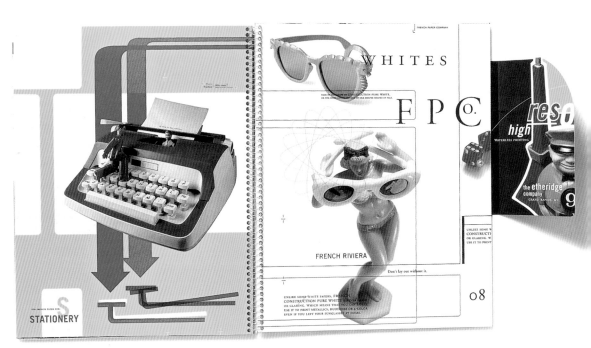

Design Firm: Pattee Design
Art Directors, Designers: Kelly Stiles,
Steve Pattee
Photographer: King Au
Copywriter: Mike Condon
Client: Fox River Paper Company

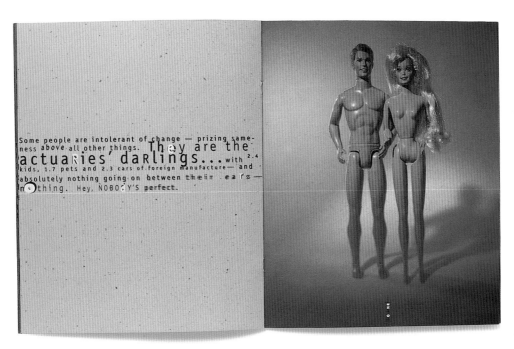

landin Paper Company, one of North America's largest producers of lightweight coated groundwood paper, created a new market segment in 1994 with the launch of INTREPID™, a paper grade with high brightness and superior opacity. In lighter basis weights – 38 to 50 lb. – INTREPID™ is more cost effective than competing grades, creating additional value for customers. A low glare version of INTREPID™ has been well-received by customers for its readability and advertising impact. A variety of major magazines and catalogs are printed on Blandin's lightweight coated paper. Blandin Paper Company, a wholly owned subsidiary of Fletcher Challenge Canada, produces approximately eight per cent of the lightweight coated paper consumed in North America each year.

Wired magazine, a specialized and growing publication in the computer field, is printed exclusively on Intrepid's low glare. Catalog publishers, like Eddie Bauer of Seattle, are major consumers of Blandin's lightweight coated paper.

A NUMBER OF MAJOR MAGAZINES AND CATALOGS AS WELL AS PRODUCT COUPONS INSERTED IN WEEKEND NEWSPAPERS ARE PRINTED ON BLANDIN'S LIGHTWEIGHT COATED PAPER.

14

15

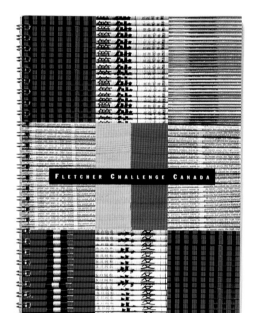

FLETCHER CHALLENGE CANADA

Design Firm: Pentagram Design
Creative Director, Art Director:
Kit Hinrichs
Designer: Amy Chan, Belle How
Illustrator: Helene Moore
Photographer: Bob Esparza
Client: Fletcher Challenge Canada, Ltd.

conomic growth in Asian countries is booming, resulting in increased consumer spending and creating demand for news and information. Like Europe, countries in Asia have distinct cultures and needs. Hong Kong, for example, is known for its free market environment, while developing economies like South Korea are just beginning to ease government regulations limiting the size of newspapers. Newsprint consumption in Taiwan has more than doubled since the 1986 removal of a regulation limiting a newspaper to three broadsheets – 12 pages. These growing economies, combined with our geographic position, provide numerous opportunities for Fletcher Challenge Canada as we expand sales of printing papers to Asian markets.

A number of noted Asian newspapers are among the most advanced in the world, achieving world-class standards for journalism, design, photography and printing technology.

FLETCHER CHALLENGE CANADA IS A MAJOR SUPPLIER OF NEWSPRINT TO MARKETS IN ASIA.

6

7

a chrysalis DREAMS

COLOR PHOTOGRAPHY OF A CATERPILLAR'S HIDDEN
BEAUTY IS BRILLIANTLY REVEALED WHEN PRINTED
4/C PROCESS ON CHALK PROTERRA FLECKS,
80# COVER.

THE BRILLIANCE OF THE BUTTERFLY'S SPOTTED WING
IS MAGNIFIED WITH A MATCH RED TOUCH PLATE.
COLOR PHOTOGRAPHY PRINTED 4/C PROCESS
ON CHALK PROTERRA VELLUM, 80# TEXT.
SHADOW PRINTS IN ONE MATCH COLOR.

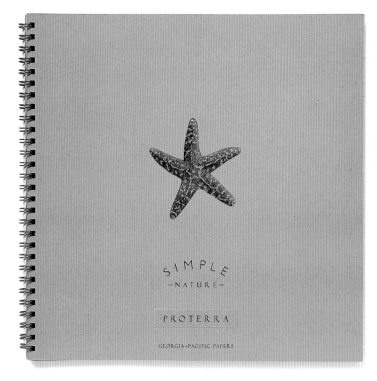

SIMPLE
—NATURE—

PROTERRA

GEORGIA·PACIFIC PAPERS

Design Firm: Leslie Evans
Design
Creative Directors: Leslie Evans,
Teresa Otul Cummings
Art Director: Leslie Evans
Designers: Leslie Evans,
Tom Hubbard,
Teresa Otul Cummings
Illustrator: Mark Gagnon
Photographer: David Sawyer
Copywriters: Liz Peavey,
Steve Treat
Client: Georgia-Pacific Corp.

THE LIVING MOMENT IS EVERYTHING.
—D.H. LAWRENCE

doesn't
see you

ust be sleeping.

COLOR PHOTOGRAPHY OF A SINGLE LEAF SHIMMERING WITH 4/C PROCESS AND A METALLIC TOUCH PLATE ON OYSTER PROTERRA VELLUM, 80# TEXT.

IN CONTRAST TO THE 4/C PROCESS, THE RUGGED TEXTURE OF THE SEA URCHIN'S DWELLING IS RECREATED IN CHILI PROTERRA FLECKS, THE COVER USING TWO METALLIC INKS AND A SCULPTURED EMBOSS.

WATERY OCEAN WORLD OF THREE SEA URCHINS IN SANDSTONE PROTERRA VELLUM, 80# COVER.

Design Firm: Sibley/Peteet Design
Designer: Don Sibley
Client: Weyerhauser Co.

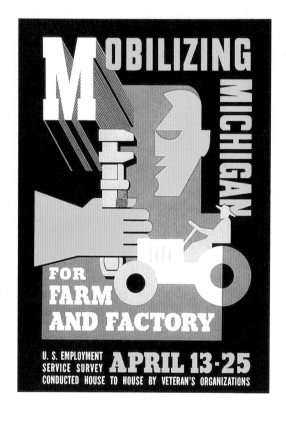

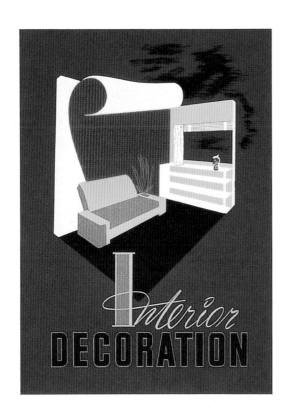

Design Firm: Pentagram Design
Creative Directors: Woody Pirtle,
Ivette Montes de Oca
Designers: Ivette Montes de Oca,
Seung Il Choi
Illustrator: Kenny Dugan
Client: Mohawk Paper Mills

ARIZONA

W 4

ND CANYON S

↑ **Flagstaff**

Albuquerque →

WEST
INTERSTATE
ARIZONA
40
↑

SIX DAYS,
1833 MILES... AND LIGHT
YEARS FROM HOME. EYES
PERMANENTLY ETCHED
BY IMAGES, & THOUGHTS IN-
GRAINED WITH STORIES
ABOUT A PLACE MORE
SURPRISING THAN ANY-
THING WE COULD HAVE
FASHIONED IN OUR DREAMS,
WE BACK FOR
FLAGSTAFF.
THEN IT'S ON TO PHOENIX
AND BACK TO WHERE
WE CAME FROM.

EAST
INTERSTATE
ARIZONA
40
→

"THEY CALL IT <u>BONY FINGERS RANCH</u>," SAID ELAINE NESBITT, "'CAUSE SINCE LOUIS PASSED, WE'VE WORKED OUR FINGERS TO THE BONE TRYING TO KEEP IT UP. LOUIS WAS THE BEST WELL-DRILLER IN THE COUNTY, BUT HE LOVED LOOKING AFTER HIS CATTLE, OVER IN THE DESERT."

"EVERY NIGHT HE'D RIDE OUT THERE, SITTING BACKWARDS ON HIS HORSE SO'S HE COULD WATCH THE SUNSET. HE BROUGHT BACK THIS MESQUITE WOOD, PIECE BY PIECE. YOU CAN'T MAKE A FENCE LIKE THIS ANYMORE. YOU CAN'T TAKE ANYTHING OUT OF THE DESERT NOW."

BIG VISTAS, TWO-LANE BLACKTOP, NOTHING BUT BLUE SKIES.
WE HEAD WEST IN SEARCH OF HIGH-OCTANE IMAGES TO SHOW THE <u>W.I.D.E.</u> OPEN POSSIBILITIES OF PHOTOGRAPHY.
ON MOHAWK NAVAJO — AND DISCOVER ANOTHER ARIZONA BETWEEN THE BLACK LINES ON THE MAP. A PLACE
WHERE CREATIVITY SOAKS YOU WITH EYE-DAZZLING CLARITY. VISION COMES IN EXTRA LARGE SIZES,
QUIRKINESS SHAKES HANDS WITH TRADITION. AND THE BEST CLICHÉ CREEPS A BLINDING GLIMPSE
OF THE OBVIOUS.
WE PACK THE VEHICLE AND HIT THE ROAD BEFORE DAYBREAK... SIPPING COFFEE... WATCHING
CONSTELLATIONS MELT INTO THE BRIGHTENING SKY. DIRE STRAITS PULSES FROM THE RADIO.
TIME EVAPORATES, MILE BY MILE... CACTUS, DRY CREEKS, OPEN RANGE, EVERYWHERE,
NOTHING BUT LIGHT... NOTHING BUT EVERYTHING.
ON THE INTERSTATE, WE SLIPSTREAM A 12 AXLE RIG AND SETTLE IN: CRUISE CONTROL FIXED
ON THE WILD SETTING, UNTIL **THIS** COMES INTO VIEW.

← **Twin Arrows**

"MAN, HOW DO THEY STAY UP.
I DON'T SEE ANY CABLES.
THEY MAKE THE DESERT SEEM EVEN
FLATTER."
TWIN ARROWS
TRADING POST IS HER FOR
SALE. I WONDER HOW MUCH IT
WOULD TAKE... IT'S REAL EASY
TO GET USED TO THE SCALE OF
THINGS OUT HERE.
WE REORGANIZE THE GEAR,
SWITCH ON THE RADAR
DETECTOR, GET READY TO
ROLL. "WHAT'S OUR NEXT
STOP?"   "WHY?"

"WHAT DO YOU MEAN... I JUST LIKE KNOWING
WHERE WE'RE HEADED."
"WHY?"
"WHY??"
"REALLY, HERE IT IS ON THE MAP. JUST SOUTH OF AJO.
   ONCE UPON A TIME IN THE WEST."

Design Firm: Miller/Huber
Relationship Marketing
Creative Director, Art Director,
Designer: Paul Huber
Editor: Doris Mitsch
Photographer: Mark Seliger
Client: Mark Seliger Photography

Michael Richards

MICHAEL AND I HAD ABOUT A ZILLION IDEAS. WE DECIDED THAT SEERSUCKERS, GOLDFISH, AND NEW YORK CITY PRETTY MUCH SUM IT UP.

Jeff Beck

THE SHEEP WERE HUNGRY, AND SOMEHOW WE KEPT GETTING MORE BUTTS THAN FACES.

Metallica

WHEN JAMES FIRST SUGGESTED THE SKULL & CROSSBONES IDEA I THOUGHT, TOO SIMPLE. AFTER THE 1ST POLAROID THOUGH, I REALIZED IT TO BE THE PERFECT HEAVY METAL IMAGE.

Red Hot Chili Peppers

WE SPENT A TON ON A STYLIST AND CLOTHING AND THIS IS WHAT WE CAME UP WITH. THE STYLIST STILL GOT CREDIT.

Mick Fleetwood & John McVie

I TOLD MICK THE IDEA, AND HE SAID, "OKAY, BUT I WANT TO BE THE ONE WEARING THE GOWN."

Ringo Starr

HE HAS SUCH A GREAT SPIRIT ABOUT HIM. HE'S THE FUNNY BEATLE.

Design Firm: Tolleson Design
Art Director: Steve Tolleson
Designers: Jean Orlebeke,
Steve Tolleson
Photographers: Everard Williams, Jr.,
Neal Brown, Hugh Kretschmer
Client: Sharpe & Associates

BOOK:

1.

SHARPE + ASSOCIATES -

VOL. I, № I

6 : 6

COLLECTIONS

TITLE   Compilation of new work
ARTISTS   SHARPE + ASSOCIATES

1.   2.   3.   4.
J.Stillings   E.Williams, Jr.   N.Brown   H. Kretschmer

SIZE   7 x 10

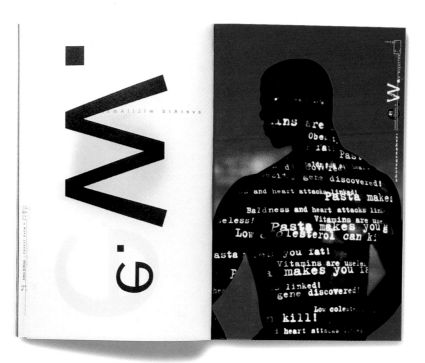

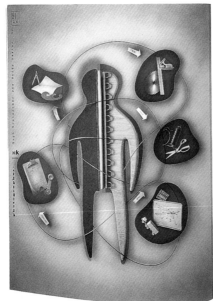

Designers: Luke Hayman, James Wojcik
Photographer: James Wojcik
Client: James Wojcik

Designers: Luke Hayman, James Wojcik
Photographer: James Wojcik
Client: James Wojcik

HIP STICKS
BRANCHES DE HANCHES
ヒップ・スティック
PALOS DE CADERA

CAPITAL EYES
YEUX CAPITAUX
YY 4663
OJOS CAPITALES

STUCK IN THE MIDDLE WITH YOU
COINCÉ AU MILIEU AVEC TOI
西村をとじこめて
AQUÍ EN EL MEDIO CON TIGO

Design Firm: Mires Design
Art Director: José Serrano
Designers: José Serrano, Eric Freedman
Photographer: Carl Vanderschuit
Client: Vanderschuit Photography

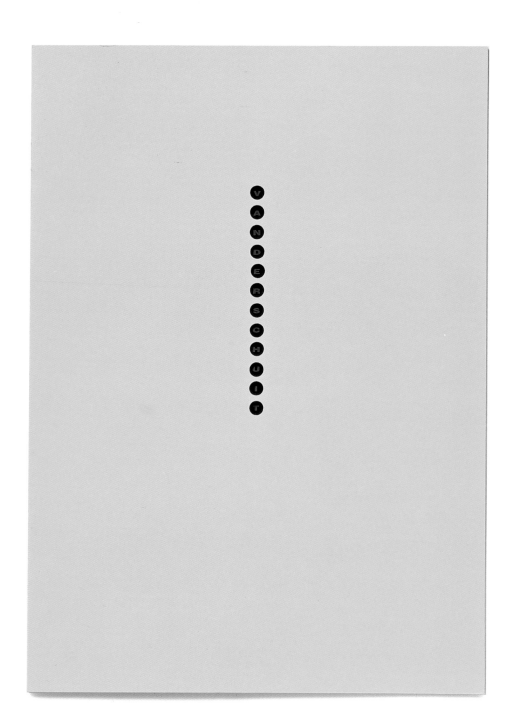

Design Firm: Saatchi & Saatchi
Business Communications
Creative Directors: Ann Hayden,
Claude Shade
Art Director: Eric Stein
Photographers: Rob Stanton,
Michael Eastman, James Schwartz
Copywriter: Todd Mitchell
Client: Eastman Kodak Co.

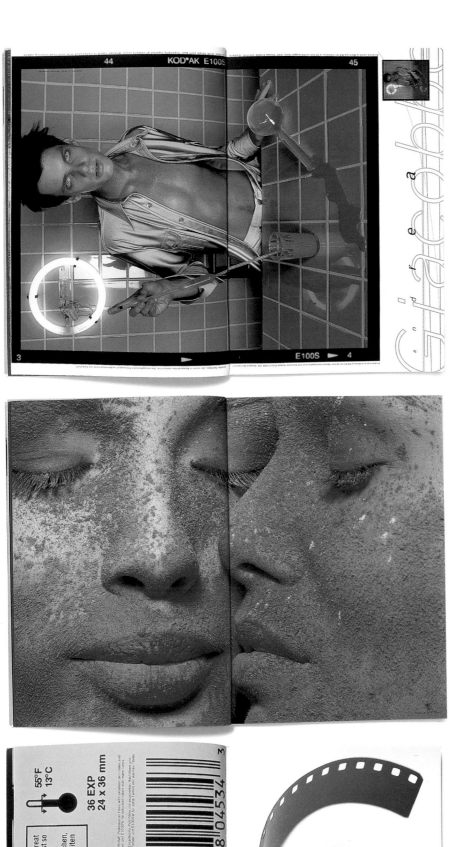

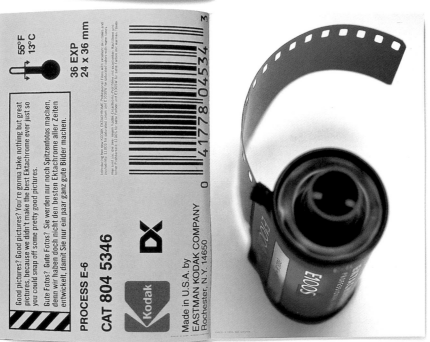

bug

Design Firm: Petrick Design
Creative Director, Art Director:
Robert Petrick
Designers: Robert Petrick, Laura Bass
Photographer: Ron Wu
Client: Consolidated Papers, Inc.

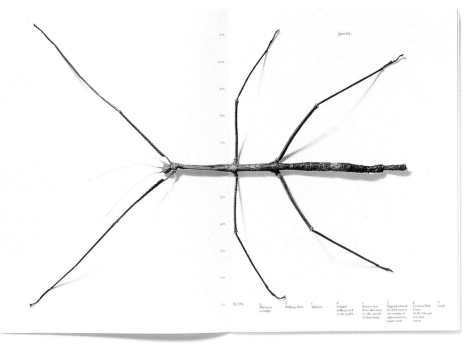

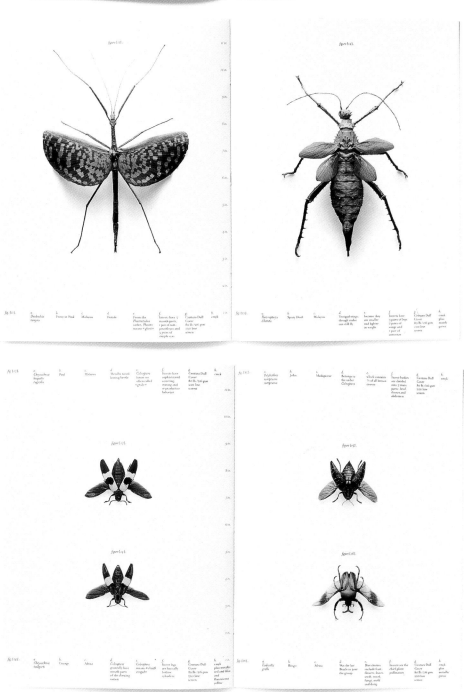

Design Firm: Robinson AD & Design
Art Director, Designer: Dana Robinson
Illustrator: Eric Spencer
Photographer: Tom Derby
Copywriter: Bruce Putterman
Client: Fox & Co.

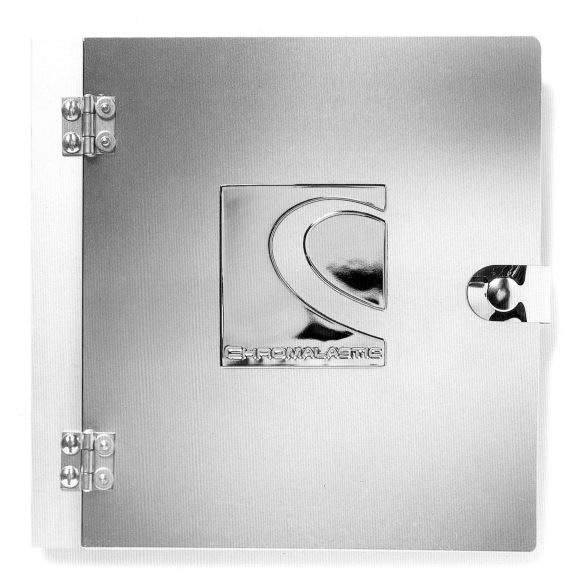

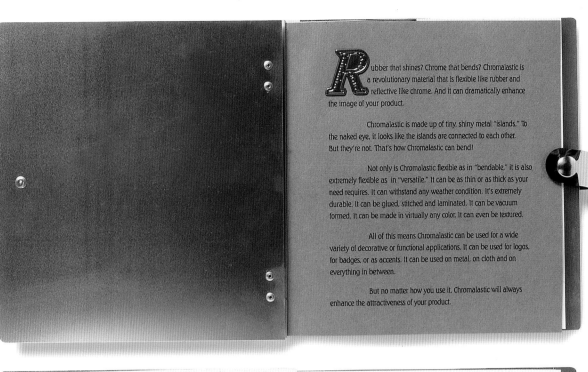

Rubber that shines? Chrome that bends? Chromalastic is a revolutionary material that is flexible like rubber and reflective like chrome. And it can dramatically enhance the image of your product.

Chromalastic is made up of tiny, shiny metal "islands." To the naked eye, it looks like the islands are connected to each other. But they're not. That's how Chromalastic can bend!

Not only is Chromalastic flexible as in "bendable," it is also extremely flexible as in "versatile." It can be as thin or as thick as your need requires. It can withstand any weather condition. It's extremely durable. It can be glued, stitched and laminated. It can be vacuum formed. It can be made in virtually any color. It can even be textured.

All of this means Chromalastic can be used for a wide variety of decorative or functional applications. It can be used for logos, for badges, or as accents. It can be used on metal, on cloth and on everything in between.

But no matter how you use it, Chromalastic will always enhance the attractiveness of your product.

Design Firm: Keller Assoziierte
Creative Director, Designer: Berud Keller
Artist: Gotthart Eichhorn
Client: Kutal

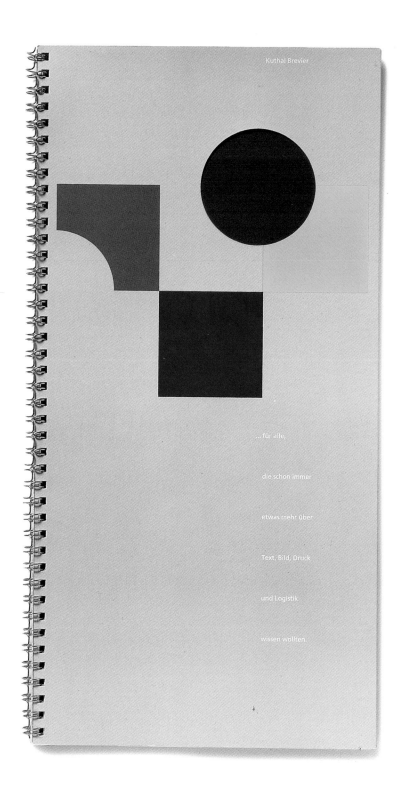

chances are

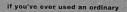

if you've ever used an ordinary

CELLULAR PHONE...

Design Firm: Petrick Design
Creative Director, Art Director:
Robert Petrick
Designers: Robert Petrick, Laura Ress
Photographer: Ron Wu
Client: Qualcomm

YOU'VE

EXPERIENCED

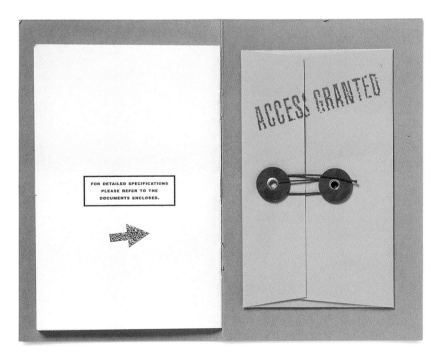

Solid Color

In schönes Blau zum Montag, ein sonniges Gelb zum grauen Sonntag oder einer freundliches Schwarz zum Freitag. Geben Sie dem Tag die Farbe, die Ihnen gefällt. „Solid Color" wurde ausgezeichnet: 1940 mit der Goldmedaille der Triennale di Milano, 1984 mit dem Design Plus Preis der Messe Frankfurt.

3

Solid Color

Vom Mokkalöffel bis zum Tafelmesser – eine glänzende Alternative zum alten Familiensilber. Aus rostfreiem Edelstahl in Frankreich geschmiedet. Klassisch in Design, variiert in 16 Farbtönen. Spülmaschinenfest.

19

Tafelgabel
Tafelmesser
Tafellöffel

Mokkalöffel
Kaffeelöffel
Kuchengabel

Salatgabel
Salatlöffel

Gemüselöffel
Fleisch-/Vorlegegabel

Saucenlöffel
Suppenschöpfer

Tortenheber

Solid Color

Teller flach 19 cm Volldekor
Teller flach Fahne
19 cm, 21 cm, 26 cm, 28 cm
Teller tief 23 cm
Platzteller 31 cm

Espresso Obere, Untere 0,10 l
Frühstück Obere, Untere 0,25 l
Cappuccino Obere, Untere 0,30 l
Jumbo Obere, Untere 0,60 l

Becher mit Henkel 0,35 l

Zuckerschale

Zuckerdose 0,30 l

Gießer 0,15 l
Krug 0,5 l, 1 l

Teekanne 0,4 l, 0,8 l, 1,1 l

Kaffeekanne 1,25 l

Eierbecher

Bol

Salatschüssel
11 cm, 15 cm, 18 cm, 22 cm

Platte oval 36 cm

Terrine mit Deckel 2,4 l

Sauciere

Salz-/Pfefferstreuer

Leuchter

Butterdose

Serviettenring

Die pure Form aus den 30er Jahren ist auch heute Leitbild für klare Gestaltung. Wo es nichts Modisches gibt, kann nichts unmodern werden. Wo alles praktisch ist, wird nichts überflüssig. Beachtung verdient auch die Qualität des Materials: hochwertiges Hartporzellan, cadmium- und bleifrei. Made in Germany.

5

Design Firm: Garza Group
Creative Director, Art Director: Agustin Garza
Designers: Agustin Garza, Vico Jimenez
Photographer: Heinz Kohler
Copywriters: Mark Winter, Agustin Garza
Client: Continental Graphics

(opposite)
Design Firm: M/W
Creative Director: Allison Muench Williams
Photographer: Geof Kern
Copywriter: Laura Silverman
Client: Takashiyama

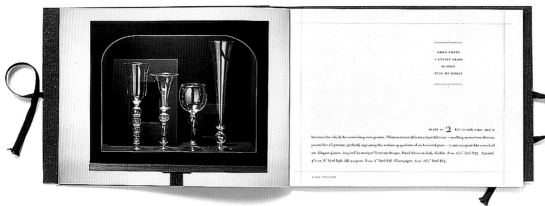

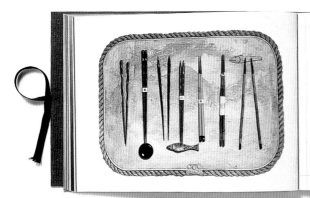

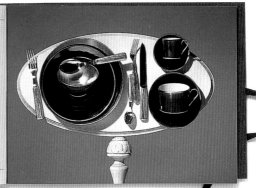

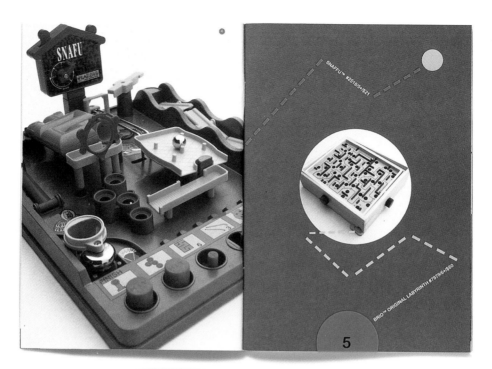

Design Firm: Sayles Graphic Design
Creative Director, Art Director, Designer:
John Sayles
Photographer: Bill Nellans
Copywriter: Mary Langen
Client: Alphabet Soup

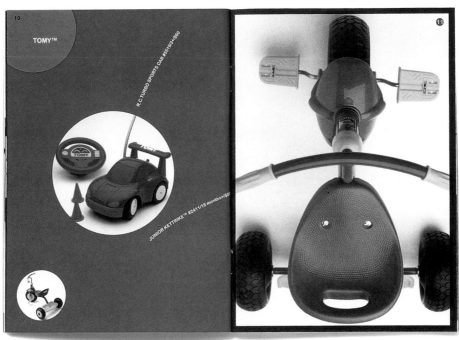

*Does your package development
usually hit the target?*

*When it comes to package development,
every advantage helps.*

Design Firm: Anderson & Lembke
Creative Director: John Athorn
Art Director: Erik Gronlund
Designer: Suzanne Lynch
Photographers: Erik Gronlund, Fred
Copywriter: Don Balser
Client: Dow Plastics

*How high have you set
your package development goals?*

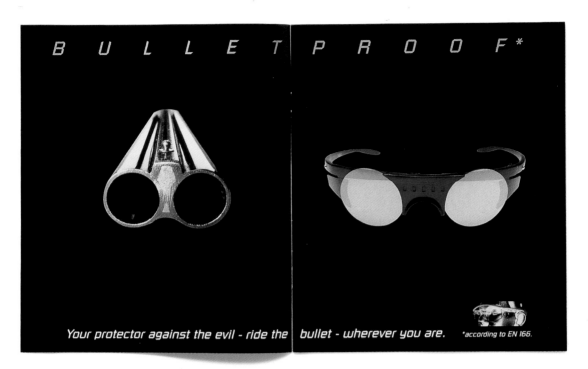

Design Firm: I-D Büro Gmbh
Art Director: Bohner/Lippert
Designers: Oliver Akrimmel/Anja Osterwalder
Photographers: Oliver Spies/
Regina Osterwalder
Client: Uvex

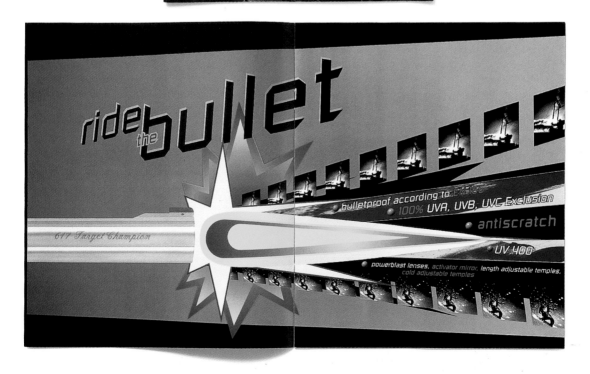

TO:

captivate

inform

interact

perform

Set your sites

Design Firm: The Leonhardt Group
Designer, Copywriter: Renée Sullivan
Photographer: Marc Carter
Client: The Leonhardt Group

We do.

ON THE INCREASINGLY CROWDED INTERNET, SOME **WEB SITES STAND OUT.**

THEY APPLY SMART **TECHNOLOGY,** CLEAR **COMMUNICATION, &** **POWERFUL DESIGN.**

The best sites create a visually dynamic image. They impart information that is immediately understood, easy to navigate, and well crafted.

The Leonhardt Group combines strong visual communication skills, technical expertise, and smart project management to develop sites that work.

We develop sites that are visually captivating, informative, and engaging. That means more hits, and longer stays.

Set your sites. Call the Leonhardt Group: 206.624.0551
For more information, visit **www.tlg.com**

Design Firm: Takenaga Design
Designer, Photographer:
Steve Takenaga
Copywriter: Kathy Takenaga
Client: Reiko M. Floral Designori

Design Firm: Takenaga Design
Designer, Photographer:
Steve Takenaga
Copywriter: Kathy Takenaga
Client: Reiko M. Floral Designori

Re:ko M.
floral designori

[248] 543.5433
fax 543.6210 734 s.washington, royal oak, mi 48067

We offer you a service that brings to you and your loved ones creative floral arrangements or fine gifts from our impressive collection.

We specialize in adding glamour and flair to home parties, corporate gatherings, special events, weddings and bar & bat Mitzvahs.

Furniture, artwork and garden ware designed by Steve Takenaga.

Offer an array of unusual containers including vintage collectibles.

We extend our sense of design to include new and exciting giftware gathered from many urban settings such as New York and San Francisco. We intermingle it with interesting vintage vases and home accessories collected from here, there and everywhere. We are able to offer you the expertise of a very innovative stuff who are able to create for you Art you'll want to live with.

Craig Frazier

Craig Frazier
Represented by Jan Collier
(415) 383-9026
(415) 383-9037 fax

Craig Frazier

As a marketer of financial services over the past 14 years, I've worn many hats. I've been a strategic planner, a manager of people, a product developer; I've overseen the creation of new corporate identities, comprehensive marketing/public relations programs and campaigns.

My experience positions me well to be a contributor to the long-term success of a progressive, innovative company.

Jack Macholl

Design Firm: VSA Partners
Art Director, Designer: Tim Bruce
Client: Jack Macholl

I'm looking for a position in which I can contribute to business success – a place to hang my hat long-term.

I'm eager to meet face-to-face to discuss my background and opportunities to make a difference for a dynamic organization.

Thank you for your consideration.

Design Firm: Batey Ads
Creative Director, Designer: Russell Fong
Artist: Jumali Katani
Copywriter: Ian Batey
Client: Batey Ads

Design Firm: Bennett Peji Design
Creative Director: Bennett Peji
Designer: Chakra Kusuma
Photographer: John Schulz
Copywriter: Bill Gerber
Client: Delectable Display

Design Firm: Bennett Peji Design
Creative Director: Bennett Peji
Designer: Chakra Kusuma
Photographer: John Schulz
Copywriter: Bill Gerber
Client: Delectable Display

The Marmoset Band's glorious music filled the air
as couples danced deep into the violet sky.
A gentle blue breeze blew wrinkled thoughts away
that admired them.
as the Pineapple fish jumped higher than the stars

Alexander stood lost as his eyes feasted on faces, on figures and feet.
"They move so swiftly, so beautifully," he thought.
Then a longing swept over him
when in the distance he caught a glimpse of sweet Sonja.

THEATER STAND

- Colors: Natural wood (maple) and Scene 3 (comes with story card)
  Dim: 16"L (span) x 17½"H x 7"W
- Authorized for Resale
  Perfect as a home fashion accessory center

Spellbound balls bounced from trees as fireworks painted the darkness.
The fountain of wine
was full all the time
and the Rosepetal pie
was delicious.
Sonja had taken
a quick rest
from the dancing
and the games
that continued
to be played
and invented.

She thought
that she'd made
all the belles of the day
and was surprised
to see a new face.
A young man stood
juggling strange shapes
by the Elephant Fountain.

"I've never seen this juggler here before," she said to herself as she moved
quickly behind a Spatdazzle tree to gain a better view.

THEATER STAND

- Colors: Scene 4 (comes with story card) and oval natural wood base (birch)
  Dim: 16"L (span) x 17½"H x 7"W
- Authorized for Resale

Design Firm: Walter Prestele/Werbung
Creative Director: Walter Prestele
Designer: Antji Bienefeld
Copywriter: Siggi Hellfutsch
Client: Can-Siggi Hellfutsch

DAS NEUE KONZEPT

DIE RICHTIGE
AGENTUR

IST IMMER NUR
SO GROSS

WIE IHRE
AUFGABEN.

DAS NEUE SPEKTRUM

FÜR

JEDEN

ANSPRUCH

GIBT ES

GANZ

IDEALE
KREATIVE.

DIE NEUE SICHT

PLÖTZLICH

IST IHR
BUDGET

M · E · H · R

WERT.

dialectdialect
dialectdialect
dialectdialect
dialectdialect
dialectdialect
dialectdialect
dialectdialect
dialectdialect

In the fertile, rolling countryside of Lancaster County, Pennsylvania, hardworking people of the Amish community speak a unique German-based dialect often referred to as Pennsylvania Dutch. The term is actually a misnomer, a corruption of the word Deutsch, or German, which forms the basis of their language.

PENNSYLVANIA

German

amishamish
amishamish
amishamish
amishamish
amishamish
amishamish
amishamish
amishamish

Design Firm: Michael Gunselman
Incorporated
Creative Director, Designer:
Michael Gunselman
Photographer: Jerry Irwin
Copywriter: Donald Prowler
Client: Fox River Paper Company

ordnung
ordnung
ordnung
ordnung
ordnung
ordnung
ordnung

lect

The Plain people, as the Amish are also known, lead a life disciplined by ORDNUNG, local church rules that set community standards in dress, decoration and behavior. Simple wardrobes are prescribed – black pants, suspenders and wide-brimmed hats for men and solid color dresses, white aprons, caps and aprons for women.

schaffdaag
schaffdaag
schaffdaag
schaffdaag
schaffdaag
schaffdaag
schaffdaag
schaffdaag

waegelche
waegelche
waegelche
waegelche
waegelche
waegelche
waegelche
waegelche

Amish life is centered around faith, community, family and a commitment to hard work. During a typical work day, or SCHAFFDAAG, all family members contribute to the best of their ability. Young children learn responsibility by caring for barnyard animals while older siblings assist in the fields or the family workshop.

Though farming is at the heart of all Amish communities, there is also a thriving tradition of craftsmanship. In Lancaster County, skilled local artisans produce simple, elegant products ranging from hand-made furniture and ironwork to WAEGELCHE, the horse-drawn buggies that are a mainstay of Plain farm settlements.

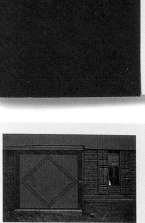

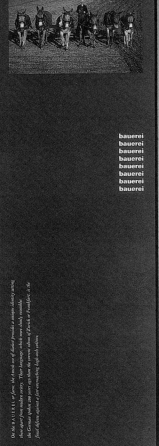

scheierdor
scheierdor
scheierdor
scheierdor
scheierdor
scheierdor
scheierdor
scheierdor

bauerei
bauerei
bauerei
bauerei
bauerei
bauerei
bauerei
bauerei

Within the strict limits of convention, the Amish demonstrate a profound love for color and design. It is evident in their handicrafts and in the deep hues and striking geometrical patterns of their world-famous quilts. Here, a traditional "center diamond" design adorns a SCHEIERDOR, the barn door of an Amish farmstead.

On the BAUEREI, or farm, the Amish use a dialect provides a unique identity setting them apart from modern society. Their language, which most chiefly remember the German (spoken some 300 years ago than the current idiom of Zurich or Frankfort), is the final defense against a fast-encroaching high-tech culture.

rumspringa
rumspringa
rumspringa
rumspringa
rumspringa
rumspringa
rumspringa
rumspringa

Adolescents are considered full members of Amish society after being baptized into the church and accepting the principles of Plain living. Before this decision, they often experience a mild rebellion called RUMSPRINGA, literally "running around." In most cases, the deviance is limited to a hunting trip with friends or sporting an ornate handkerchief.

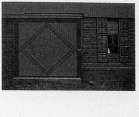

Design Firm: Tinguely Concept
Creative Director, Designer: Johann Terrettaz
Photographer/Illustrator: David Schender
Client: Niedecker Snowboards

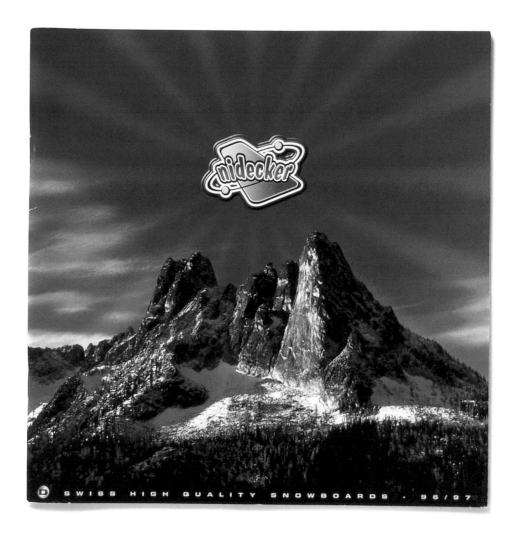

CONCEPT

Legende und Kult. Nideckers super leichtgängige Carving-Maschine, die konzipiert wurde um Nidecker's weltweiter Bekanntheit beigetragen. Das Concept hat von allen Boards bisher am meisten zu Slalomweltmeister ins Ziel zu tragen. Das Nidecker Worldcup Race-Team fährt Serienboards.

MODEL	54	60	66
TOTAL LENGTH (cm)	154	160	166
EFFECTIVE EDGE	1300	1345	1370
NOSE WIDTH (cm)	252	262	276
MIN. WIDTH (cm)	195	202	214
TAIL WIDTH (cm)	247	256	264
RADIUS R/F	12/7.8	13.4/2	7.4/6.4
# INSERTS	16	16	16
STANCE (cm)	430	456	476
OFFSET	30	31	32
NOSE RADIUS	280	280	280
TAIL RAD.	235	235	235

DESIGNED FOR: FREECARVING

NIDECKER

EXTREME SL

Nicht alles was symmetrisch aussieht ist symmetrisch. Denn innere Asymmetrie erlaubt extrem schnellen, griffigen Kantenwechsel die äußere optische Symmetrie sorgt für extreme Laufruhe. Anfänger Finger weg. Hier gibt's nasse Hosen und blaue Flecken. Das Extreme ist ein reines Freecarve und Slalom Raceboard. Das Nidecker Worldcup Race-Team fährt Serienboards.

MODEL	46	52	58
TOTAL LENGTH (cm)	146	152	158
EFFECTIVE EDGE	1280	1230	1300
NOSE WIDTH (cm)	235	246	257
MIN. WIDTH (cm)	180	190	200
TAIL WIDTH (cm)	230	241	252
RADIUS R/F	12/7.5	7.4/4	9.3/6.3
# INSERTS	16	16	16
STANCE (cm)	430	456	476
OFFSET	29	30	31
NOSE RADIUS	260	260	260
TAIL RAD.	235	235	235

DESIGNED FOR: RACING

softs 1

[a] 700:
Bindung mit Alu-Grundplatte. Sehr komfortables 3D gespritztes Highback. "One Strap fits all" System.

[b] 800:
Bindung mit Alu-Grundplatte. Viele Möglichkeiten zur individuellen und präzisen Einstellung. Ideale Freeride Bindung.

[c] 900:
Bindung mit Carbon-Epoxy-Glass Platte. Gleiches Gewicht wie eine Baseless Bindung. 4x4 Lochung 360 Grad verstellbar. Dämpfung an Grundplatte. Der Fixierriemen mit EVA Schaum und ein Schnellverschluß garantieren ein präzises und schnelles Schließen der Bindung. Die Schnellöffnungs-Ratsche entläßt den Boarder augenblicklich vom Gerät.

softs 2

[a] 200:
Junior Bindung wie beim Erwachsenenmodell. Dünnere 3mm Alu-Grundplatte. Schnellverschluss und öffnung. Leicht auf alle Größen verstellbar.

[b] 400:
Fiberglas verstärkte Plastik-Grundplatte in ergonomischer Form. Sehr starker Alu-Ring, 4x4 Lochung, Schnellverschluss und öffnung. "One Strap fits all" System.

[c] 500:
Baseless Bindung für besseren Kontakt zum Board. Dampfung, Mittelhoher Spoiler, 4x4 Lochung.

JASON

Im fernen Vermont steht Champ Jason weiter hinter seinen beiden "U.S. Style"-Boards. Eines ist sehr kurz und breit für "stylische" Pisten-Tricks. Das andere ist länger und fürs entspannte Freeriding gedacht.

Jason Evans 47

MODEL	47	54
TOTAL LENGTH (cm)	147	154
EFFECTIVE EDGE	1128	1140
NOSE WIDTH (cm)	233	245
MIN. WIDTH (cm)	252	256
TAIL WIDTH (cm)	283	256
RADIUS R/F	9	9.5
# INSERTS	20	20
STANCE (cm)	530	536
OFFSET	25	30
NOSE RADIUS	320	320
TAIL RAD.	320	320

BABS

Unter der Anleitung von Babs Charlet entwickelten wir sein Board weiter. Ein "Skate-Style"-Board für den Worldcup-Einsatz. Gebaut für weiche Landungen und Flat Tricks. Jedoch machen die zurückgesetzten Inserts auch den Tiefschnee-Traum wahr. Der ideale Kompromiß zwischen Pipe und Freeriding.

MODEL	51
TOTAL LENGTH (cm)	1516
EFFECTIVE EDGE	1216
NOSE WIDTH (cm)	294
TAIL WIDTH (cm)	294
RADIUS R/F	6.5
# INSERTS	20
STANCE (cm)	530
OFFSET	30
NOSE RADIUS	320
TAIL RAD.	320

DESIGNED FOR: FREESTYLE

Design Firm: Slaughter Hanson
Creative Director: Terry Slaughter
Art Director, Designer: Marion English
Photographers: John Huet, Don Harbor
Copywriter: Laura Holmes
Client: Friends of Rick Wood

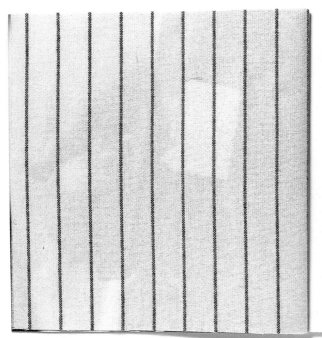

ON A SULTRY HOT AUGUST 18, 1910, THE CITY WAS STRANGELY SILENT. SOMETHING BIGGER THAN BUSINESS WAS GOING ON OUT IN WEST END. SOMETHING BIG ENOUGH TO DRAW 10,000 CITIZENS OUTDOORS AND ACROSS TOWN ON A SWELTERING SUMMER AFTERNOON. THE COMING OF THIS EVENT HAD CAPTIVATED AN ENTIRE CITY. AND AT 3:00 THAT AUGUST AFTERNOON, THE MOMENT CAME. WITH THE PITCH OF A BASEBALL, ONE YOUNG MAN PLACED A GLEAMING NEW DIAMOND IN BASEBALL'S CROWN. RICKWOOD FIELD. THIS GEM OF A PARK WOULD ONE DAY BE THE LAST REMNANT OF THE GLORIOUS EARLY DAYS OF BASEBALL. ALL THE OTHER GREAT PARKS OF THAT DAY WOULD SEE BASEBALLS GIVE WAY TO WRECKING BALLS, AND RICKWOOD WOULD STAND ALONE, BASES LOADED WITH HISTORY, AS THE OLDEST BASEBALL PARK IN AMERICA.

TODAY, AFTER YEARS OF SITTING IDLE, COVERED IN THE DUST OF TIME AND PROGRESS, RICKWOOD FIELD IS BEING RESTORED TO THE DAZ- ZLING DIAMOND OF ITS EARLY DAYS. MORE THAN JUST PRESERVING AN HISTORIC STRUCTURE, WE ARE CREATING A PLACE TO RELIVE THE MAGIC OF BASEBALL'S GLORY YEARS. WHY BOTHER? READ THE PAPERS. WATCH THE NEWS OF THE GAME. FIND, IF YOU CAN, THE PASSION OF THE GAME AMERICA FELL IN LOVE WITH FROM THE START. WITH EACH OF THE OLD GRANDSTANDS THAT FELL, IT SEEMS, WE LOST MORE THAN JUST AN OLD, OUTDATED STRUCTURE. WE LOST A BIT OF ROMANCE. A BIT OF WONDER. A BIT OF ALL THAT IS TRULY GOOD ABOUT AMERICA. AND SO, FOR THOSE HOPELESS ROMANTICS WHO ARE STILL IN LOVE BUT A LITTLE DISENCHANTED WITH THE GAME, WE ARE PRESERVING RICKWOOD FIELD. OUR DREAM IS FOR RICKWOOD FIELD TO BE A WORKING MUSEUM, A PLACE TO ACTUALLY SEE AND EXPERIENCE BASEBALL AS IT ONCE WAS.

YOU KNOW, THEY SAY THAT WHEN A BASEBALL LEGEND DIES HIS SPIRIT PLAYS ON FOREVER. IF THAT IS TRUE, THEN RICKWOOD FIELD MUST BE HEAVEN. FOR SO LONG, THE GOLDEN DAYS OF BASEBALL HAVE SURVIVED ONLY IN THE HEARTS AND MINDS OF THOSE WHO LOVE THE GAME. BUT AT RICKWOOD FIELD, THE EXPERIENCE OF THOSE DAYS LIVES AGAIN IN THE FLESH. NOT ONLY ARE WE REKINDLING THE ROMANCE IN THE BALLPARK ITSELF, BUT THERE WILL BE A BASEBALL MUSEUM IN THE FUTURE AS WELL. THIS MUSEUM WILL BRING THE RICKWOOD LEGENDS TO LIFE, AND WILL HOUSE SOUTHERN

LEAGUE AND NEGRO AMERICAN LEAGUE MEMORABILIA, BRINGING VISITORS FACE TO FACE WITH THE WAY IT USED TO BE. FROM THE ACTUAL BATS THAT SWUNG THE COURSE OF HISTORY TO THE UNIFORMS THAT OUTFITTED MERE MEN FOR THEIR JOURNEY INTO IMMORTALITY, TO THE ORIGINAL PHOTOS AND PUBLICITY THAT EMBLAZONED THEIR IMAGES IN OUR MINDS, IT WILL ALL BE HERE, BRINGING TO LIFE THOSE DAYS THAT ARE OTHER- WISE ALL BUT LOST. IF YOU TRULY LOVE BASEBALL, THIS COULD VERY WELL BE THE CLOSEST YOU'LL EVER GET TO HEAVEN ON EARTH.

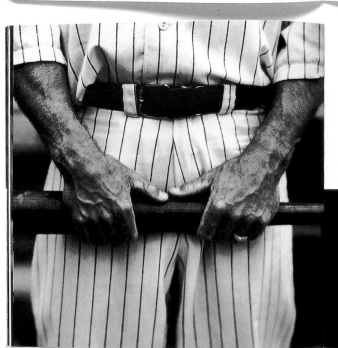

THE
MUSEUM

Design Firm: BlackBird Creative
Creative Director: Patrick Short
Designer, Photographer,
Illustrator: Brandon Scharr
Copywriter: Curtis Smith
Client: Pinehurst Country Club & Resort

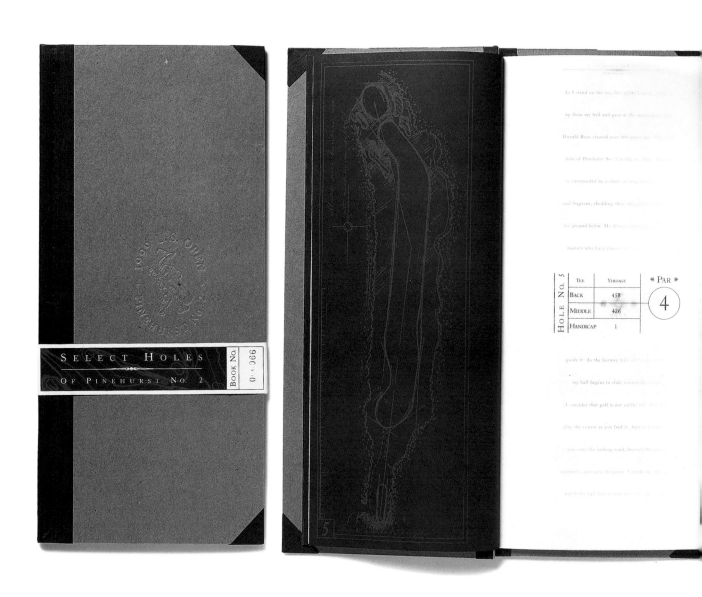

(opposite)
Design Firm: Elton Ward Design
Creative Director, Art Director:
Jason Moore
Designer: Justin Young
Photographer: Natalie Arditto
Client: Australian Design Awards

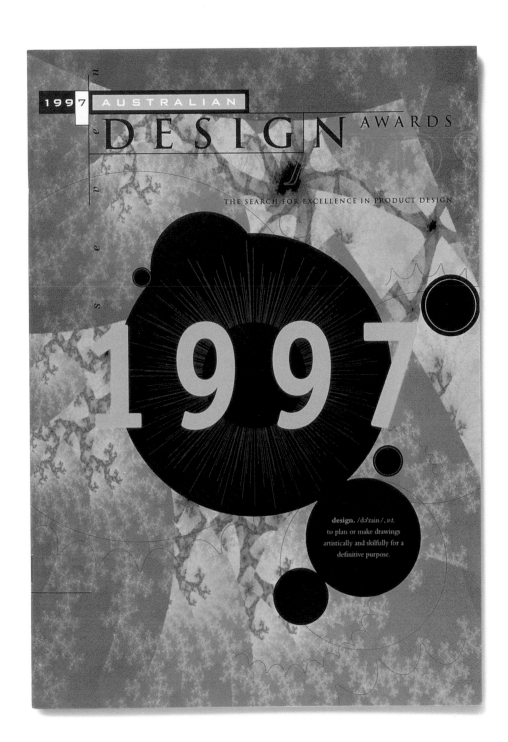

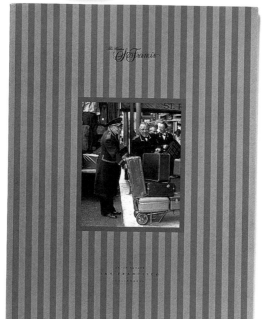

Design Firm: Arias Associates
Creative Director, Art Director:
Mauricio Arias
Designers: Mauricio Arias,
Steve Mortensen
Photographer: Robert Miller
Copywriter: Words by Design
Client: The Westin St. Francis

GUEST SUITES

For an intimate gathering or a small meeting, our specialty suites and parlor suites are the perfect choice. Like all of our guest rooms, they too have been recently renovated to reflect The St. Francis style. With classic furnishings and serene colors, these suites have played host to royalty, heads of state, literary figures, and film personalities. The St. Francis Suite on the 12th floor was the home of three legendary San Francisco families for more than 30 years. In 1983, President and Mrs. Reagan were guests during their historic visit with Queen Elizabeth and Prince Philip, who stayed in the now famous Windsor Suite.

Milk Bath

When theater impresario Florenz Ziegfeld announced to the press in the early 1900s that his wife, Anna Held, would only bathe in 30 gallons of fresh milk, he set off a nationwide fad that had women across the country touting the merits of the now-famous St. Francis milk baths. Each night, the press reported that Anna would go up to her room followed by a caravan of waiters carrying bottles of milk. Not long after Anna Held left The St. Francis, the reigning family of American theater, the Barrymores, moved in. They too were pampered by The St. Francis staff. Ethel Barrymore's pet chimpanzee was looked after without question. But it was not just socialites who received a warm welcome at The St. Francis—so too did the new music of the time called jazz. Although other hotels had signs warning guests that 'jazz dancing' was not acceptable, The St. Francis was encouraging it with the likes of Art Hickman and his orchestra playing in the White and Gold Room. The room was later renamed The Rose Room after Hickman's famous hit of the same name.

Wine and Beverage List
· 1933

Money Laundering

Since 1938, The Westin St. Francis has operated the world's only silver coin cleaning operation as a favor to its guests. This custom began when the hotel's manager insisted that the silver coins—the currency of the day—be cleaned to keep the ladies' white gloves from getting dirty. Periodically, the change is collected, washed and polished in a silver-burnishing machine, rinsed off and dried under hot lights, then carried back to the front desk. For more than 31 years, Arnold Batliner laundered The St. Francis money—he cleaned an estimated $17 million in change. Today, every taxi driver and cashier in San Francisco knows that if they get mint-clean money, it's probably from The St. Francis.

Design Firm: The Campbell Group
Creative Director: Cristina Creager
Art Director: Joanne Westerman
Copywriter: Jeff Grutkowaski
Client: Metropolitan Washington
Airports Authority

FOR A

VISION

to be fully

REALIZED

it must be SHARED

THE NEW TERMINAL

at Washington National Airport

IS A

triumph of unity.

This evening,
the creation of **the New**
Terminal *comes to fulfillment as*
WE OPEN ITS DOORS TO YOU —
THE PEOPLE WHO TURN TO
Washington National Airport
for safe and timely transport.
Thank you *for being here tonight.*
Thank you for sharing
in this CELEBRATION.

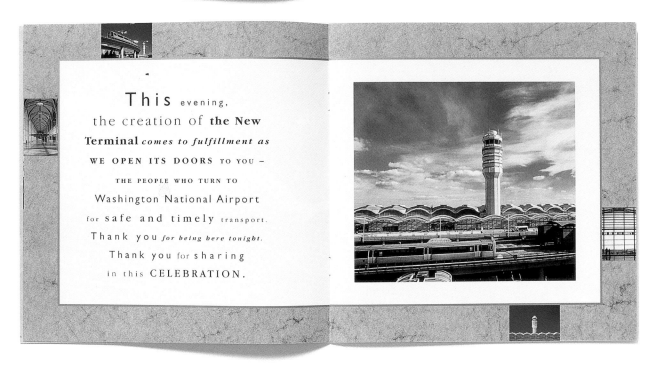

Design Firm:
ZaNon Design Communication
Creative Director: Ciriano Zanon
Designer: Mara Biasia
Client: Lotto Calzature SPA

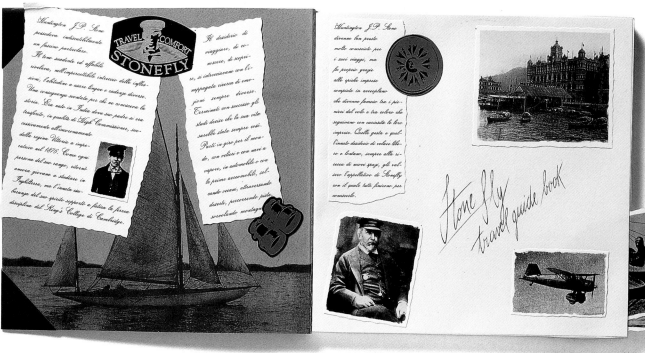

(opposite)
Design Firm: BlackBird Creative
Creative Director, Designer:
Patrick Short
Photographer: Martin Fox
Illustrator: Jack Unruh
Copywriter: Lori McNabb
Client: Black Mountain/
Swannanoa Chamber of Commerce

In turn-of-the-century music halls, renowned entertainers perform Bluegrass, Jazz, Acoustical Folk, and Classical.

Nearly 50 antique dealers send you on a scavenger hunt through America's attics, for everything from country

collectibles to heirloom pieces. Discover the town's creative side with contemporary arts and crafts.

Take on America's longest municipal par 6 (747 yards). The area's beauty and serenity offer a retreat for the

Explore
BLACK MOUNTAIN
North Carolina

How to get Lost in a Town with only one Main Street.

soul, a natural setting for the large number of religious conference centers. If your body is in need of a rest, settle down in a charming bed and breakfast or cozy inn.

Black Mountain, North Carolina, is a great place to lose yourself. And don't worry. We have plenty of maps.

Located along the Hand Made in America Craft Heritage Trail, Black Mountain is just one block north of I-40. A short drive from Asheville, Biltmore Estate, Lake Lure, Chimney Rock and the Blue Ridge Parkway. For help planning your vacation, write or phone the Black Mountain/Swannanoa Chamber of Commerce Visitors Center

Black Mountain
800-669-2301
Black Mountain/Swannanoa Chamber of Commerce Visitors Center

Black Mountain/Swannanoa Chamber of Commerce Visitors Center
201 East State Street, Black Mountain, NC 28711
www.blackmountain.org   www.blackmountain-nc.com

Smoke away the stresses of daily life at the Andromeda Health and Beauty Centre. Aromatherapy, Reflexology and Thalassotherapy rejuvenate the mind and body. Pamper yourself with a massage. Unwind in the sauna, jacuzzi or steam bath. Enjoy The Annabelle's two tennis courts, squash court, fitness room, as well as a full range of water sports.

Design Firm: David Carter Design Assoc.
Creative Director: Lori B. Wilson
Art Director, Designer: Sharon LeJeune
Photographer: Henri D'Olmo
Copywriter: Melissa Gatchel North
Client: The Annabelle-Thanos Hotels

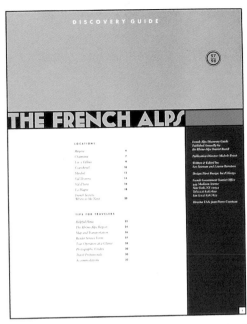

Design Firm: Pivot Design, Inc.
Creative Director, Art Director:
Brock Haldeman
Designer: Brock Haldeman, Jim Larmon
Illustrator: Paul Cox
Copywriter: Rania Haldeman
Client: French Government Tourist Office

Design Firm:
Slaughter Hanson
Creative Director,
Designer:
Marion English
Copywriter:
Laura Holmes
Client: Plainclothes

1
0
1
0
1
0
1
0

It has been 10 years now since we first stepped out in pursuit of our dream of PlainClothes. ◆ And what a remarkable experience it has been. ◆ At every turn, we have crossed paths with the most intriguing people. ◆ Almost daily, we stumble upon unforeseen challenges, each presenting new opportunities for growth and creativity. ◆ Here, to celebrate our 10th Anniversary, we recall 10 such encounters which have made a great adventure out of this venture we call PlainClothes.

X

T E N

1
0

T
H
A
T

is it!"I felt my face getting flushed and my jaw clenching as I signed the parcel delivery slip. ◆ Yet another day

BLANKET EXCUSES
—————————
CALIFORNIA

and another delivery had passed without the arrival of our long-awaited shipment.

The new season was quickly approaching. Our regular clientele had already begun asking for this particular line of clothing. But our supplier had not yet come through.

This delay was totally unexpected. The designer is a woman we trust and respect implicitly. Her line of women's clothing is beautifully crafted of wonderful, rich fabrics in irresistibly flattering shapes. We love the clothing. Our clients love the clothing. And, we had always received prompt, conscientious fulfillment of every order.

But this time, we had no merchandise. We had waited. And waited. Now, we could wait no more.

I snatched up the phone and dialed the number. I had to answer to my customers. Today I was

Indices **Verzeichnis** Index

Creative Directors Art Directors Designers

Photographers Illustrators Writers

DesignFirms Agencies

Clients

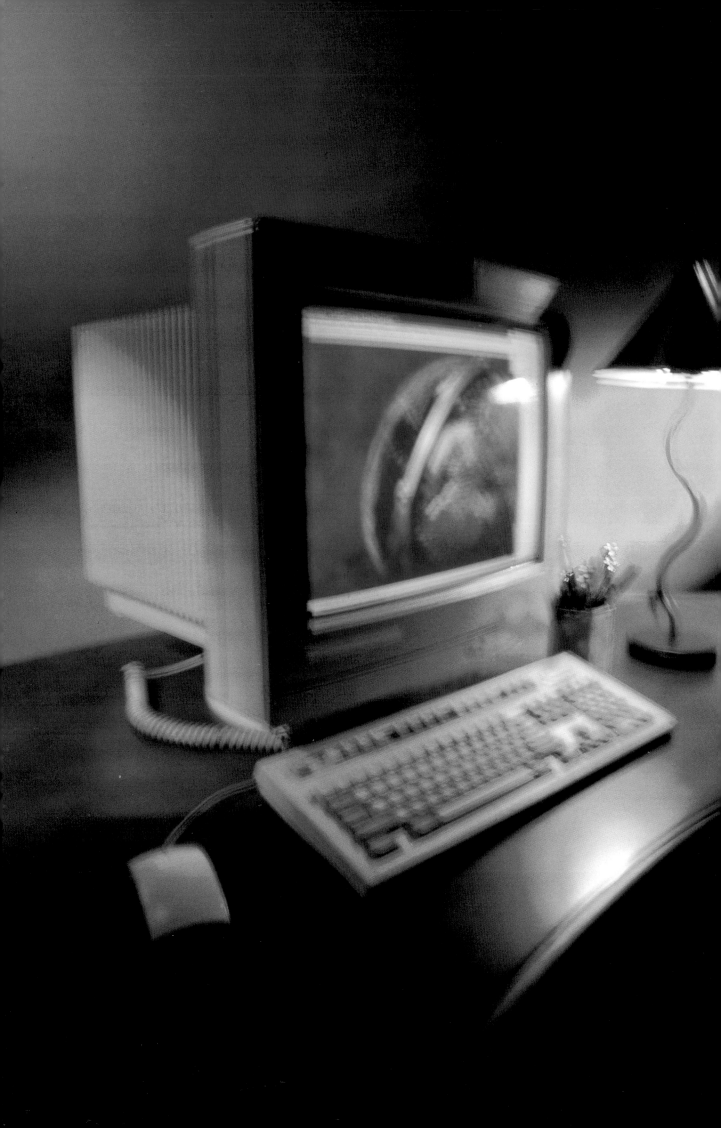

Order Graphis on the Web from anywhere in the world: www.graphis.com

GRAPHIS 313

GRAPHIS 314

GRAPHIS 315

GRAPHIS 316

Subscribe to our
Magazine and save
40% on all Books!

Poster Annual 1998

Corporate Identity 3

Book Design 2

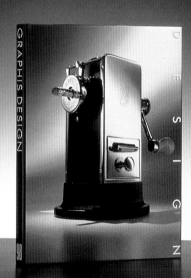

New Talent Design Annual 1998

GRAPHIS PRODUCT DESIGN

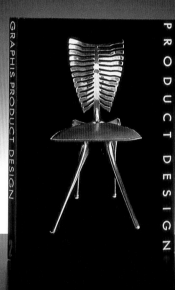

PRODUCT DESIGN

T-shirt Design 2

GRAPHIS DESIGN

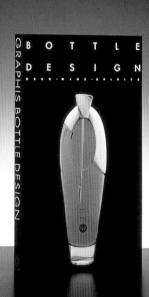

GRAPHIS BOTTLE DESIGN

BOTTLE
DESIGN

AppleDesign

The Work of the Apple Industrial Design Group

Order Form

As a subscriber to the magazine, you automatically qualify for a *40 percent discount* on any of our books. If you place a standing order you will receive a *50 percent discount*. This means any Graphis book you select is sent to you as soon as it comes off press, and you will be billed at half the cover price plus shipping. With a *standing order* Graphis doesn't have to go through the expense of contacting you by mail and can therefore pass the savings directly back to you. Our annuals such as Poster, Photo, Design, and Advertising come out every year. The rest of our books come out every 2-4 years. If you don't wish to receive a particular book automatically when it happens to come out just choose the *40 percent off price*. If you are not a subscriber, then you still receive a *20 percent discount*. For your support we now cover all the communication disciplines and if there is a Graphis book you care to have that is not listed, please call us and we will do everything we can to get it for you. We thank you for your support.

Book Title	Retail	Non Subscriber 20% off	Subscriber 40% off	Standing Order 50% off	Quantity	Totals	Book Title	Retail	Non Subscriber 20% off	Subscriber 40% off	Standing Order 50% off	Quantity	Totals
Spring Books 1998							**General Interest**						
Book Design 2	☐$70	☐$56	☐$42	☐$35			**Nudes 1**	☐$40	☐$32	☐$24	☐$20		
Corporate Identity 3	☐$70	☐$56	☐$42	☐$35			**Nudes 2**	☐$50	☐$40	☐$30	☐$25		
New Talent 1998	☐$60	☐$48	☐$36	☐$30			**Passion & Line**	☐$50	☐$40	☐$30	☐$25		
Poster Annual 1998	☐$70	☐$56	☐$42	☐$35			**Pool Light**	☐$70	☐$56	☐$42	☐$35		
T-Shirt 2	☐$60	☐$48	☐$36	☐$30			**Typography 2**	☐$70	☐$56	☐$42	☐$35		
Fall Books 1998							**Walter Iooss**	☐$70	☐$56	☐$42	☐$35		
Advertising 1999	☐$70	☐$56	☐$42	☐$35			**Design Books**						
Annual Reports 6	☐$70	☐$56	☐$42	☐$35			**Apple Design**	☐$45	☐$36	☐$27	☐$23		
Brochures 3	☐$70	☐$56	☐$42	☐$35			**Bottle Design**	☐$40	☐$32	☐$24	☐$20		
Design Annual 1999	☐$70	☐$56	☐$42	☐$35			**Magazine Design**	☐$70	☐$56	☐$42	☐$35		
Digital Photo 1	☐$70	☐$56	☐$42	☐$35			**Products by Design 1**	☐$70	☐$56	☐$42	☐$35		
Letterhead 4	☐$70	☐$56	☐$42	☐$35			**Products by Design 2**	☐$70	☐$56	☐$42	☐$35		
Logo Design 4	☐$60	☐$48	☐$36	☐$30			**Web Design Now**	☐$70	☐$56	☐$42	☐$35		
Photo Annual 1998	☐$70	☐$56	☐$42	☐$35									

Shipping & handling per book, US $ 5.00, Canada $ 10.00, Elsewhere $15.00		
New York State shipments add 8.25% tax		
☐ I am not a subscriber, but I want to qualify for the 20% off discount.		

Graphis Magazine	USA (shipping included)	Canada (shipping included)	International (shipping included)	International (airmail surcharge included)
One year subscription, 6 Issues	☐ $90	☐ $100	☐ $125	☐ $184
Two year subscription, 12 Issues	☐ $165	☐ $185	☐ $235	☐ $294
Student subscription, 6 Issues	☐ $59	☐ $59	☐ $80	☐ $139

☐ I am presently a Graphis magazine subscriber and therefore, qualify for the 40% discount.

Total

Name	☐ American Express ☐ Visa ☐ Mastercard ☐ Check
Company	
Address	Card #
City State Zip	Expiration
Daytime phone	Card holder's signature

Copy or send this order form and make check payable to Graphis Inc. For even faster turn-around service, or if you have any questions about subscribing call us at the following numbers in the **US (800) 209. 4234, outside the US (212) 532. 9387 ext. 242 or 241, Fax (212) 696. 4242. Graphis 141 Lexington Avenue New York, New York 10016-8193. Order Graphis on the Web from anywhere in the world: www.graphis.com**

Graphis Books Call For Entry

If you would like us to put you on our Call for Entries mailing list for any of our books, please fill out the form and check off the specific books of which you would like to be a part. We now consolidate our mailings twice a year for our spring and fall books. If information is needed on specific deadlines for any of our books, please consult our web site: www.graphis.com.

Graphic Design Books	☐ Poster Annual	**Photography Books**	**Student Books**
☐ Advertising Annual	☐ Products by Design	☐ Digital Photo (Professional)	☐ Advertising Annual
☐ Annual Reports	☐ Letterhead	☐ Human Con. (Photojournalism)	☐ Design Annual
☐ Book Design	☐ Logo Design	☐ New Talent (Amateur)	☐ Photo Annual (Professional)
☐ Brochure	☐ Music CD	☐ Nudes (Professional)	☐ Products by Design
☐ Corporate Identity	☐ New Media	☐ Nudes (Fine Art)	☐ **All the Books**
☐ Design Annual	☐ Packaging	☐ Photo Annual (Professional)	☐ All Design Books only
☐ Digital Fonts	☐ Paper Promotions	☐ Photography (Fine Art)	☐ All Photo Books only
☐ Diagrams	☐ Typography		☐ All Student Books only

First Name: _____   Last Name: _____

Company: _____

Telephone: _____   Fax: _____

Mailing Address: _____   City: _____

State, Country: _____   Zip: _____

Copy or mail form to : Graphis, Call for Entries, 141 Lexington Ave., New York, New York 10016-819, USA, or fax to 212. 213 3229

INTERNATIONAL PAPER: A PAPER LOVE STORY THAT BEGAN 100 YEARS AGO.

It started as a pulp and paper company based in the Northeastern part of the United States. Now, 100 years later, International Paper is a world-class company with manufacturing operations in 31 countries throughout the world.

On January 28, 1898, representatives from 17 pulp and paper mills met and agreed to form International Paper. Three days later, on January 31, the incorporation papers were filed in Albany, New York.

During its early years, International Paper was the nation's largest producer of newsprint, supplying 60 percent of all newsprint sold in the U.S. and exporting to Argentina, England and Australia.

Hugh Chisholm served as president of International Paper from 1898 to 1907 and under his leadership, the first laboratory in the American pulp and paper industry was constructed.

The Great Depression of the 1930s was a difficult period for International Paper. To help weather the hard times, International Paper introduced new products and branched out into the packaging business. International Paper was one of the first companies to manufacture linerboard on the Foudrinier. (The original Foudrinier, invented in 1799 and later perfected in 1801, allowed paper to be made in continuous rolls instead of one sheet at a time).

In 1939, International Paper pioneered bleached kraft grades for folding cartons, tags, and file folders and supplied the first bleached kraft paper grades suitable for milk carton production.

In 1941, the company simplified its structure and during World War II, International Paper converted some manufacturing operations to produce military items that included the V-1 box, which replaced wooden crates for shipping military supplies.

International Paper saw unprecedented growth and prosperity after World War II. The company had no debt and expanded its landholdings, more than doubling its fee-owned lands from 2.5 million to 5.8 million acres. To enhance forest management and research, International Paper developed its professional forestry services, established a research laboratory at Mobile, Alabama, and developed the "Super Tree" through selective breeding of genetically superior pine trees.

In 1955, the company launched a multimillion dollar research program to develop the plastic-coated milk carton. It also formed the International Paper Company Foundation, a grant-making organization that supports education in International Paper communities. Today, the foundation supports various environmental, civic, cultural, and health programs throughout the United States.

International Expansion

International Paper expanded outside the U.S. in the late 1950s. It had been a major exporter for decades with sales in London, Paris, Zurich and Johannesburg. Still, in 1959, with over $1 billion in sales, International Paper added the first overseas manufacturing operations through joint ventures with container companies in Israel, Germany, Greece, and Italy. That same year, it organized a new subsidiary and built a liquid-packaging plant in Caracas, Venezuela.

International Paper continued its international expansion throughout the 1960s and in 1969, the Corporate Research Center at Sterling Forest, New York was built.

A large scale corporate reorganization in 1976 replaced the Southern Kraft and The Northern Divisions with functional business units: white papers, consumer packaging, industrial packaging, wood products, and speciality packaging. Production managers were encouraged to think like marketing and financial managers, as well.

During the 1980s, International Paper launched a quality program that focused employees on customer needs giving them opportunities to improve product quality and to help redistribute decision-making authority throughout the organization. The company also introduced a variety of new products, including Classic Pak which captured a 20 percent share of the poultry market.

International Paper acquired Hammermill, referred to as the "best-known name in paper," which had a distribution network and reputation for quality unrivaled in the American pulp and paper industry. Its distribution network became the foundation for ResourceNet International, now called xpedx.

The Move to Memphis

International Paper moved its headquarters to Memphis, Tennessee in 1987 to be closer to the mills and other facilities. During the 1980s, the company had strengthened its position in speciality markets by investing in businesses that were related to its core business but less cyclical in earnings than the pulp and paper market. In 1985, they took ownership of Arizona Chemical, a leading global supplier of pulp chemicals. Three years later, they acquired Maonite Corporation, a manufacturer of hardboard wood products like door facings.

As the decade came to a close, the company continued to increase its international holdings. In 1989, International Paper acquired Zanders Feinpapiere AG, Germany's leading producer of coated papers that was founded in 1829, and Aussedat Rey, a diversified French manufacturer of office copying paper, speciality panels, and related products that dated back to the 18th century.

Then in 1992, International Paper acquired Kwidzyn, Poland's most modern paper mill. This was the first acquisition in eastern Europe after the end of the Cold War.

By 1995, International Paper was a major shareholder in Carter Holt Harvey of New Zealand, which operated in New Zealand and Australia. International Paper also owns part of COPEC, a Chilean energy and forestry company.

In 1996, Federal Paper Board teamed with International Paper in a $3.5 billion transaction. Later that year, International Paper opened the new Cincinnati Technology Center that develops improvements in printing, packaging, and extrusion coating.

By 1996, sales reached $20 billion and today 85,000 employees make International Paper a global leader and a company of choice for both customers and shareholders.

In 1997, Zanders, Aussedat Rey, and Strathmore Beckett integrated their European speciality paper divisions to form a new company called International Paper Premium Papers (IPPP).

The complete range of speciality products from Aussedat Rey mills at Robertsau, Strasbourg, and Lana Docelles, as well as the Zanders mills of Reflex and Gohrmühle form the group. Yet, the American Strathmore Beckett products are still offered as an independent franchise from their European headquarters in the Netherlands.

International Paper is committed to becoming an organization with a strong customer focus and a greater degree of teamwork in order to satisfy customers and stay ahead of the competition. As Chairman John Dillon said recently, "I can think of no other company in the industry with more capacities to meet these objectives than ours. We are proud of what we have achieved in 100 years and look forward to greater success in the future."

INTERNATIONAL PAPER: HUNDERT JAHRE LIEBE ZUM PAPIER

Alles begann mit einer Zellstoff- und Papierfirma im Nordosten der Vereinigten Staaten. Heute, 100 Jahre später, ist International Paper ein Unternehmen der Weltklasse mit Produktionsstandorten in 31 Ländern rund um die Welt.

Am 28. Januar 1898 trafen sich Vertreter von 17 Zellstoff- und Papierfabriken und vereinbarten die Gründung von International Paper. Drei Tage später, am 31. Januar 1898, wurde das Unternehmen in Albany im Staat New York angemeldet.

In den ersten Jahren war International Paper der größte amerikanische Hersteller von Zeitungspapier mit einem Marktanteil von 60 Prozent, wobei auch nach Argentinien, England und Australien exportiert wurde.

Von 1898 bis 1907 war Hugh Chisholm Präsident von International Paper. Unter seiner Führung wurde das erste Labor der amerikanischen Zellstoff- und Papierindustrie gebaut.

Die große Depression in den dreißiger Jahren war auch für International Paper eine schwere Zeit. Um sich in dieser schwierigen Lage zu behaupten, führte International Paper damals neue Produkte ein und diversifizierte in das Verpackungsgeschäft. Dabei gehörte International Paper zu den ersten Firmen, die kaschierten Karton auf der Foudrinier-Maschine herstellten. (Mit der Foudrinier-Maschine, die 1799 erfunden und 1801 weiterentwickelt wurde, konnte Papier erstmalig in durchlaufenden Rollen statt jeweils nur in einem Bogen hergestellt werden.)

1939 war International Paper wegweisend mit gebleichten Kraftpapiersorten zur Herstellung von Faltschachteln, Etiketten und Aktenordnern und lieferte die ersten gebleichten Kraftpapiersorten, die für die Produktion von Milchtüten geeignet waren.

Nach dem Krieg erfuhr International Paper ein noch nie dagewesenes Wachstum und einen beispiellosen Wohlstand. Das Unternehmen hatte keine Schulden und verdoppelte seinen Grundbesitz von 1 Million Hektar auf 2,3 Millionen Hektar. Zur Verbesserung der Forstverwaltung und -forschung entwickelte International Paper einen eigenen professionellen Forstbereich, errichtete in Mobile, Alabama ein Forschungslabor und entwickelte den „Superbaum" durch selektive Zucht genetisch überlegener Nadelbäume.

1955 startete das Unternehmen ein Forschungsprogramm mit einem Budget von vielen Millionen Dollar für die Entwicklung der kunststoffbeschichteten Milchtüte. Zusätzlich wurde die International Paper Company Foundation gegründet, eine Stiftung zur Förderung der Bildung in den Standortgemeinden von International Paper. Heute finanziert die Stiftung vielfältige Programme im Bereich Umwelt, Soziales, Kultur und Gesundheit in den gesamten USA.

Internationale Expansion

In den späten fünfziger Jahren expandierte International Paper auch außerhalb den Vereinigten Staaten. Seit Jahrzehnten war der Export ein wichtiger Umsatzfaktor, besonders nach London, Paris, Zürich und Johannesburg. Im Jahre 1959, als International Paper einen Jahresumsatz von über einer Milliarde Dollar hatte, wurden mit Behälterfirmen in Israel, Deutschland, Griechenland und Italien Gemeinschaftsunternehmen und somit die ersten Fertigungsstätten im Ausland gegründet. Im gleichen Jahr wurde eine neue Tochtergesellschaft eröffnet und eine Verpackungsanlage für Flüssigbehälter in Caracas in Venezuela errichtet.

Die internationale Expansion von International Paper wurde in den sechziger Jahren fortgeführt. 1969 wurde das Forschungszentrum des Konzerns in Sterling Forest im Staat New York gebaut.

Im Jahre 1976 wurden die Sparten Southern Kraft und Norther durch die folgenden Funktionsbereiche ersetzt: Weißpapier Komsumverpackung, Industrieverpackung, Holzprodukte un Spezialverpackung. Die Produktionsleiter waren angewiesen, sich auch die Denkweise von Marketing- und Finanzmanagern anzueignen. In den achziger Jahren startete International Paper ein Qualitätsprogramm, das die Mitarbeiter auf die Bedürfnisse der Kunden ausrichtete, den Mitarbeitern die Möglichkeit zu Verbesserung bot und dazu beitrug, die Entscheidungsfindung au das gesamte Unternehmen zu verlagern. Weiterhin führte da Unternehmen mehrere Neuprodukte ein, zum Beispiel Classic Pak das 20 Prozent des Geflügelmarktes eroberte.

International Paper erwarb Hammermill, das den Ruf des „am beste bekannten Papiernamens" besitzt und für das überlegen Vertriebsnetz und die herausragende Qualität in der amerikanische Papier- und Zellstoffindustrie berühmt ist. Das Vertriebsnetz vo Hammermill wurde der Grundstein für die Firma ResourceNe International, die ab 1. Januar 1998 unter xpedx firmierte.

Umzug nach Memphis

Im Jahre 1987 verlegte International Paper die Konzernzentrale nach Memphis, um näher bei den Papierfabriken und den anderen Werken zu sein.

Das Unternehmen stärkte in den achziger Jahren seine Position au Spezialmärkten, indem gezielt in Firmen investiert wurde, die mi dem Kerngeschäft des Konzerns zu tun hatten, jedoch weniger konjunkturabhängig als der Zellstoff- und Papiermarkt waren. 198 übernahm International Paper die Firma Arizona Chemical, ein weltweit führender Lieferant von Zellstoffchemikalien. Drei Jahr später folgte der Kauf der Maonite Corporation, die Holzfaserplatten produkte wie z.B. Türverkleidungen herstellt.

Am Ende des Jahrzehnts folgten internationale Übernahmen. 1989 wurde Zanders Feinpapiere AG, der führende deutsche Hersteller von gestrichenen Papieren, sowie Aussedat Rey, ein diversifizierter französischer Produzent von Kopierpapier, Spezialplatten und ähnlichen Produkten, erworben. Zanders wurde 1829 gegründet, während die Anfänge von Aussedat Rey bereits im 18. Jahrhunder liegen.

Am Ende 1996 erzielte International Paper einen Umsatz von 20 Milliarden Dollar. Heute ist International Paper mit 85.000 Mitarbeitern ein Weltführer der Branche und sowohl für Kunden als auch Aktionäre eine erste Adresse.

1997 bildeten Zanders, Aussedat Rey und Strathmore Beckett in Europa mit ihren Spezialpapierbereichen ein neues Unternehmen namens International Paper Premium Papers (IPPP).

Die gesamte Palette von Spezialprodukten der Papierfabriken von Aussedat Rey in Robertsau, Straßburg und Lana Docelles sowie die Reflex- und Gohrsmühle-Fabriken von Zanders wird die Gruppe bilden. Die Produkte der amerikanischen Hersteller Strathmore und Beckett werden weiterhin unabhängig von der europäischen Zentrale in Holland vertrieben.

International Paper hat sich das Ziel gesetzt, ein kundenorientiertes Unternehmen mit mehr Teamarbeit zu werden, um so Kundenwünsche erfüllen und den Wettbewerb schlagen zu können. So sagte der Vorstand John Dillon neulich: „Ich kenne kein anderes Unternehmen in der Branche, das diese Ziele besser erreichen könnte als wir. Wir sind stolz darauf, was wir in 100 Jahren erreicht haben, und freuen uns auf einen noch größeren Erfolg in der Zukunft."

INTERNATIONAL PAPER: UNE HISTOIRE D'AMOUR AVEC LE PAPIER QUI A COMMENCÉ VOICI UN SIÈCLE

Tout commence avec une manufacture de pâte et de papier située dans le nord-est des Etats-Unis. Aujourd'hui, 100 ans plus tard, International Paper est une société d'envergure mondiale qui possède des sites de fabrication dans 31 pays du monde.

Le 28 janvier 1898, les représentants de 17 manufactures de pâte et de papier se réunissent et tombent d'accord pour créer International Paper. Trois jours plus tard, le 31 janvier, la société nouvellement formée est enregistrée à Albany, New York.

Au cours de ses premières années d'activité, International Paper est le principal fabricant de papier journal du pays. En effet, il fournit 60 % du papier journal vendu aux Etats-Unis et exporte vers l'Argentine, la Grande-Bretagne et l'Australie.

Hugh Chisholm préside International Paper de 1898 à 1907 et c'est à cette époque que l'on construit le premier laboratoire de l'industrie américaine de la pâte et du papier.

Pendant la Grande Crise des années 30, International Paper connaît une période difficile. Pour parvenir à surmonter la tempête, International Paper lance de nouveaux produits et se diversifie dans le secteur de l'emballage. International Paper est une des premières entreprises à fabriquer des cartons sur le Foudrinier. (Le Foudrinier d'origine, inventé en 1799 et perfectionné en 1801, permet de produire le papier en rouleaux et non plus feuille par feuille).

En 1939, International Paper commercialise pour la première fois du papier kraft blanchi de qualité supérieure pour cartons pliables, étiquettes et porte-documents et fournit le premier papier kraft blanchi adapté à la fabrications des emballages de lait.

International Paper connaît une croissance et une prospérité exceptionnelles après la Seconde Guerre. L'entreprise n'a pas une seule dette et fait plus que doubler ses biens fonciers puisqu'ils passent de 2,5 millions à 5,8 millions d'acres (n.d.t. : 1 acre = 0,405 hectares). Pour améliorer la gestion des forêts et la recherche, International Paper développe ses services forestiers professionnels, établit un laboratoire de recherches à Mobile, Alabama et met au point le „super tree" par croisements sélectifs d'espèces de pins supérieures.

En 1955, la société lance un programme de recherches qui porte sur plusieurs millions de Dollars pour mettre au point un emballage de lait en carton doublé de matière plastique. Elle fonde également la Paper Company Foundation, un organisme chargé d'attribuer des bourses d'étude dans les communes où elle est implantée. Aujourd'hui, la Fondation supporte différents projets dans le secteur de l'environnement, de la vie civile, dans le domaine de la culture et de la santé à travers les Etats-Unis.

Expansion internationale

International Paper développe ses activités hors des Etats-Unis à la fin des années 50. Société exportatrice de tout premier plan pendant des décennies, International Paper a des point de vente à Londres, Paris, Zurich et Johannesbourg. En 1959, alors que ses ventes atteignent plus de 1 milliard de Dollars, la société acquiert ses premiers sites de fabrication outre-mer par le biais de joint ventures en Israël, Allemagne, Grèce et Italie. La même année, elle crÈe une nouvelle filiale et construit une usine de conditionnement des liquides à Caracas, Venezuela. International Paper poursuit son expansion internationale tout au long des années 60. En 1969, elle construit le Corporate Research Center à Sterling Forest, N.Y.

Une vaste opération de restructuration conduit, en 1976, au remplacement de Southern Kraft et des Northern Divisions par des unités fonctionnelles correspondant aux secteur suivants : papier blanc, conditionnement consommateur, conditionnement industriel, produits en bois et emballages spéciaux. Les directeurs de production sont invités à ne pas oublier les aspects commerciaux et financiers. Au cours des années 80, International Paper lance un programme qualité qui attire l'attention des collaborateurs sur les besoins du consommateur, leur donne la possibilité d'améliorer la qualité des produits et encourage la prise de décisions à tous les échelons de l'organisation. La société introduit également toute une variété de nouveaux produits, y compris Classic Pak qui conquiert 20 % du marché de la volaille.

International Paper achète Hammermill, encore appelée „le meilleur nom du papier," avec son réseau de distribution et sa réputation de qualité inégalée dans l'industrie américaine de la pâte et du papier. Son réseau de distribution met en place le ResourceNet International, en vigueur depuis le 1er janvièr 1998 sous le nom de xpedx.

Le déménagement à Memphis

International Paper établit son quartier général à Memphis en 1987 pour se rapprocher des manufactures et des autres équipements.

La société renforce sa position sur le marché des spécialités au cours de années 80 en investissant dans des affaires liées à son activité principale mais moins sujettes aux fluctuations cycliques que la pâte et le papier. En 1985, elle acquiert Arizona Chemical, un des premiers fournisseurs de produits chimiques pour la pâte à papier. Trois ans plus tard, elle achète la Masonite Corporation qui fabrique des panneaux durs pour parements de portes, par exemple.

Vers la fin de la décennie, la société continue à accroître ses possessions internationales. En 1989, International Paper reprend Zanders Feinpapiere AG, le premier producteur allemand de papiers couchés et Aussedat Rey, un fabriquant français de papiers de tirage à usage de bureau, de plusieurs gammes de spécialités et de produits annexes. Zanders a été fondé en 1829 alors que la naissance de Aussedat Rey remonte au 18e siècle.

En 1996, les ventes atteignent 20 milliards de Dollars et aujourd'hui, 85 000 collaborateurs font de International Paper un leader universel et une entreprise de tout premier choix pour les clients et les actionnaires.

En 1997, Zanders, Aussedat Rey et Strathmore Beckett unissent leurs secteurs européens des spécialités de papier pour former une nouvelle société appelée International Paper Premium Papers (IPPP). La gamme complète des spécialités de la manufacture Aussedat Rey à Robertsau, Strasbourg et Lana Docelles, ainsi que la manufacture Zanders de Reflex et Gohrmühle constitueront le groupe. Les produits américains de Strathmore Beckett sont toujours proposés en franchise indépendante par le quartier général européen situé aux Pays-Bas.

International Paper est destinée à devenir une organisation largement orientée vers les consommateurs et à renforcer son esprit d'équipe pour satisfaire les clients et devancer la concurrence. Comme le disait récemment son Président John Dillon: „Je ne vois aucune autre entreprise industrielle qui posséderait plus d'atouts que nous pour réaliser ces objectifs. Nous sommes fiers de ce que nous avons obtenus en 100 ans et nous nous attendons à un succès encore plus grand à l'avenir."

STRATHMORE - BECAUSE PAPER IS PART OF THE PICTURE

When Horace Moses founded the Mittineague Paper Company in West Springfield, Massachusetts back in 1892, the memories of the Wild West were still fresh in the minds of many. Perhaps that is why he named his paper factory–Mittineague–after an Indian tribe which had once inhabited the area.

Moses' company philosophy was just as simple as it was convincing: He wanted to produce unusually high quality paper and offer an outstanding service. He was constantly searching for new paper machines with which he could manufacture unusual types of paper. He had heard that there was a machine in England that could produce deckle-edges similar to those of handmade paper. He travelled to Europe and not only did he find the machine but also a name for his products in Scotland: Strathmore.

The picturesque valley of Strathmore with its heather and Scottish thistle in full bloom left a lasting impression on Moses. In 1898, he registered the name "Strathmore" as a trademark and chose the thistle as his company's logo.

Horace Moses was convinced that he could sell his products well if he were to display the beauty of his paper in many different ways. And so he went down in American design history as the publisher of the first sample book with practical examples. For this purpose, he employed his own printer in his company: Will Bradley, who later became renowned the world over as a typography designer and printer of high quality books.

The customers were thrilled with the sample books and the paper too. The company expanded. New acquisitions included an envelope factory which ensured that there were matching envelopes for the different paper types, and all of famous Strathmore quality.

Horace Moses died in 1947 at age 85. He left a legacy, but the following management generations were not always gifted with his keen business sense. In 1962, Strathmore was sold to Hammermill and since 1986 has belonged to the largest paper conglomerate in the world: International Paper.

THE PRODUCT RANGE

Today, Strathmore is a leading supplier in three special areas:

Paper containing cotton

In paper with a 25% share of cotton, Strathmore is market leader in the USA. This is predominantly due to the Strathmore Writing System. Originally developed at the end of the eighties, this system was recently revised and adapted to market conditions. Thanks to technical improvements, the paper can be used without any problems on all laser printers. In addition to different degrees of white, the colour selection also includes neutral shades which are produced using a high content of recycled material. These colors give the impression of colored paper but can be as flexibly used as white paper.

Text and cover papers

Strathmore is known above all for its colored envelope qualities. Authentic felt marks are the trademark of this paper factory. The qualities Grandee, Americana, Fiesta and Pastelle are still manufactured on the old paper machines which almost work at a manual pace. Many factories have already given up this technology in favor of faster production processes. Strathmore, in contrast, is constantly working on adapting these special features to the demands of the modern market.

Artist's paper

Strathmore is also the market leader in the USA for artist's paper. This paper is offered in a range stretching from 100% cotton paper to types made fully out of wood.

This paper can be bought solely in the USA through specialist retailers in sheets or as artist's blocks.

A MODERN MARKETING CONCEPT

Strathmore's main target is the graphic design community, which plays a decisive role in choosing paper and expresses great interest in new paper qualities and application examples. The trend is moving away from pure sample books towards combined sample and application books. The latter show examples with different printing techniques: thermography, blind blocking, foil laminating, and dye stamping. Unusual impressions can thus be attained on weighty natural papers. The application books include detailed technical information with regard to lithography, printing, and further processing. The advantage of this system is obvious: it provides a huge source of ideas without the risk of taking a shot in the dark when putting them into practice.

Strathmore also provides specialist advice to avoid that "shot in the dark." Since 1958, Strathmore has been training the "Graphic Arts Consultants" of the sales partners, paper wholesalers in 35 countries around the world. Strathmore provides a seminar, lasting several days, which teaches the agency consultants about the role of paper in graphic design, different printing techniques, as well as the latest trends in paper and design. Special consultants often provide advertising agencies with ideas and information which the printers cannot provide due to a lack of time or in-depth knowledge.

Strathmore caters to the needs of the advertising agencies in its product range. A complete program is offered for every type of paper, i.e several different weights of paper and card, as well as envelopes and matching stickers.

Strathmore's European headquarters is located in Bussum in the Netherlands. From this location the European wholesalers receive sales support especially matched to their market. As the headquarters has its own warehouse, products can be delivered within a few days.

THE NEWEST TRENDS

Extensive market research has shown what people really want with paper, what trends will continue through 2000. Emphasis is of course placed on environmental friendliness. This is why at Strathmore, depending on the quality required, only paper with a maximum recycling content is produced. The use of cotton is also ecologically sound, as this is a raw material which grows back quickly. And what's more, in paper production, only the outer layers of cotton unsuitable for textile production are used. Another trend is that paper has to meet the demands of modern office printers and state-of-the-art fast printing machines. To this end, a relatively smooth closed surface and a special moisture content are required and the paper should also be available in A4 format. And last but not least, the advertising agencies require that high quality paper be affordable. The result of these findings has a name at Strathmore: Elements—an environmentally friendly composition of materials (60% recycling share), factory guaranteed suitability for laser printers (up to 105 g/m2), and a cost of about 10% less than comparable papers.

Elements was developed by product manager Bob Daigneault together with the New York advertising agency Designframe. Six soft pastel shades and the basic elements of graphic design—lines, dots, squares, grid, grain and zigzag—give Elements its new exciting look. Tests have shown that the patterns incorporated in the paper are visible or disappear depending on the thickness and covering power of the printing inks used. If the sample is just visible, it supplements the print in such a way that interesting effects in the printing image can be attained without the colored structure of the paper appearing overpowering or distracting. An interesting interaction between paper and print also develops. And, there is also a neutral version (solids).

Jim Sebastian from Designframe drew up a sample book which interprets the linguistic use of the design elements in funny graphics (e.g. square headed). Sebastian is very impressed by Strathmore and says of their relationship: "Working together with a paper manufacturer enables designers to advance art." To date, this cooperation was only limited to sales promotion. By jointly drawing up elements ranging from the conception to the market positioning, a truly new path is being taken. Horace Moses certainly would have approved.
—Gabriele Eisenbarth, May 1998

THE STRATHMORE GRADES

Americana

Americana's beautiful, pronounced surface, achieved by combining an authentic marking felt with a dandy roll pattern, is unique among text and cover papers. It is receptive to all printing and finishing techniques including four-color process, engraving, foil stamping, and dye cutting. It is particularly dramatic with embossing. Available in an array of acid-free whites, Americana comes in text and cover grades.

Grandee

Richly textured Grandee offers exceptional choice, with four recycled, acid-free whites, a range of recycled colors, two virgin fiber colors, and four recycled duplex combinations. Grandee combines an authentic felt finish with a dandy roll pattern. Its outstanding opacity and ink holdout make it ideal for four-color process as well as all other printing and finishing techniques.

Fiesta

Strathmore Fiesta is an acid-free, deckle-edged sheet now offered with the same authentic felt finish as Strathmore Pastelle. Its deckle edge is uniquely rendered in a choice of seven colors on white. By dressing up the envelope flap, the deckle is an excellent way to increase the overall impact of announcements and greeting cards. Fiesta is available in Text 80 (118g/qm) and in Cover 80 (216g/qm).

Pastelle

With its subtle texture and deckle edge, Strathmore Pastelle offers a wide range of opportunities for creativity. Its fresh palette features three whites, one gray, and four soft colors. Authentic felt-finished, acid-free Pastelle is receptive to all printing and production techniques. Its high opacity, superior ink holdout, and deckle edge make it especially suited for social correspondence and high-end marketing communications.

Rhododendron

A durable 25% cotton sheet with unique Telanian finish, Rhododendron offers the look and feel of handwoven Irish linen. It is available in three acid-free whites, three grays, black, and four sophisticated colors. Rhododendron's 25% cotton content provides extra strength and durability for all applications. Its surface is exceptional for four-color process as well as for all other printing and production techniques.

Renewal

Strathmore Renewal text and cover is a premium recycled paper containing 25% post-consumer and 25% pre-consumer recovered material by total fibre weight. The seven solid and seven fibre enhanced colors coordinate with each other in hue. The wove surface is ideal for all printing and production processes, from 4-color process, engraving and foil stamping to die cutting, embossing and scoring. Outstanding ink holdout and opacity make it ideal for all types of distinctive communication when quality and environmental concern are equally important.

Writing System

This system offers a selection of fine correspondence papers from the Strathmore Writing System, America's most comprehensive and distinctive paper system for printed communications. Engineered to meet the needs of business into the next century, the Strathmore Writing system offers an unparalleled selection of virgin content and recycled, acid-free papers in coordinating finishes and colors. The writing weights of Strathmore Writing, Strathmore Pure Cotton, and Strathmore Script are backed by the Strathmore Laser Guarantee, ensuring their reliable performance in copy machines and laser printers.

Elements

Strathmore Elements has an exceptionally smooth, level surface which guaranties excellent printability. The patterns are created with papermaking dyes applied by a unique manufacturing process. A solid version is also available. Six subtle colors were carefully designed to complement and coordinate with each other. The colors also coordinate with Strathmore Writing. This paper is an ideal choice for all printing and finishing techniques, from 4-color process, engraving and foil stamping to dye cutting, embossing, and scoring.

STRATHMORE - WEIL PAPIER VIEL ZUM IMAGE BEITRÄGT

Die Zeiten des „Wilden Westens" waren in den Köpfen durchaus noch lebendig, als Horace Moses 1892 die Mittineague Paper Company in West Springfield, Massachusetts, gründete. Vielleicht benannte er seine Papierfabrik deshalb nach dem Indianerstamm, der in die-sem Gebiet einmal gelebt hatte.

Moses´ Firmenphilosophie war ebenso einfach wie über-zeugend: Er wollte außergewöhnliche, hochwertige Papiere produzieren und einen herausragenden Service bieten. Ständig suchte er nach neuen Papiermaschinen, mit denen er ausgefallene Sorten fertigen konnte. Er hatte davon gehört, daß es in England eine Maschine gab, die Büttenränder produzieren konnte, die handgeschöpftem Papier sehr ähnlich waren. Er reiste nach Europa, fand die Maschine und in Schottland auch gleich den Namen für seine Produkte: Strathmore.

Das landschaftlich wunderschöne Valley of Strathmore, in dem die Heide und die schottischen Disteln gerade in voller Blüte standen, hatte einen bleibenden Eindruck bei ihm hinterlassen. 1898 ließ er den Namen „Strathmore" als Warenzeichen eintragen und die Distel wurde zum Firmenlogo.

Horace Moses war davon überzeugt, daß er sehr gute Verkaufserfolge erzielen könnte, wenn er die Schönheit seiner Papiere in vielfältiger Weise zeigte. So ging er als Herausgeber des ersten Musterbuches mit Anwendungsbeispielen in die amerikanische Design-Geschichte ein. Er beschäftigte bei sich im Hause dafür eigens einen Drucker: Will Bradley erlangte später als Typographie-Designer und Drucker von hochwertigen Büchern Weltruhm.

Die Kunden nahmen die Musterbücher und so auch die Papiere mit Begeisterung auf, das Unternehmen expandierte. Unter den Neuerwerbungen befand sich auch eine Briefumschlagfabrik, die sicherstellte, daß es zu den einzelnen Papierqualitäten die passenden Umschläge in bekannter Strathmore Qualität gab.

Horace Moses starb 1947 im Alter von 85 Jahren, und die nachfolgenden Geschäftsführer erwiesen sich nicht immer als ebenso genial. 1962 wurde Strathmore an Hammermill verkauft und gehört seit 1986 zum größten Papierkonzern der Welt: International Paper.

DIE PRODUKTPALETTE

Heute ist Strathmore ein führender Anbieter auf drei Spezialgebieten:

Baumwollhaltige Papiere

Bei den Sorten mit 25 % Baumwollanteil besitzt Strathmore in den USA den größten Anteil.

Dafür ist in erster Linie das Strathmore Writing System verantwortlich. Es wurde Ende der achtziger Jahre entwickelt und soeben vollständig überarbeitet und den Markterfordernissen angepaßt. Technische Verbesserungen machen einen problemlosen Einsatz auf allen Laserdruckern möglich. Die Farbpalette bietet außer verschiedenen Weißegraden auch „farbige Neutraltöne" an, die mit einem hohen Recyclinganteil hergestellt werden. Diese Farbtöne erwecken zwar den Eindruck eines farbigen Papieres,

sind jedoch so flexibel einsetzbar wie ein weißes Papier.

Text und Cover Papiere

Bekannt ist Strathmore vor allem für seine farbigen Umschlagqua litäten. Authentische Filzmarkierungen sind das Markenzeichen dieser Papierfabrik. Die Qualitäten Grandee, Americana, Fiesta und Pastelle werden noch immer auf alten Papiermaschinen gefertigt die beinahe im Handwerkertempo arbeiten. Viele Fabriken haben diese Technik bereits zugunsten wesentlich schnellere Produktionsprozesse aufgegeben. Strathmore arbei-tet hingegen ständig daran, diese Besonderheiten den Anforderungen des modernen Marktes anzupassen.

Künstlerpapiere

In den USA ist Strathmore Marktführer bei Künstlerpapieren. Die werden in einer Bandbreite von 100% Baumwollpapier bis zu komplett holzhaltigen Sorten angeboten. Als Bogenware oder als Zeichenblock kann man diese Pa-piere ausschließlich in den USA im Facheinzelhandel kaufen.

Ein modernes Marketingkonzept

Strathmore wendet sich in erster Linie an Grafikdesigner. Die haben einen entscheidenden Anteil bei der Papierauswahl und sind daran interessiert, stets neue Papierqualitäten und Anwendungsbeispiele zu erhalten. Der Trend entwickelt sich weg von reinen Papiermusterbüchern hin zu kombinierten Muster-und Anwendungsbüchern. Letztere zeigen Beispiele mit unterschiedlichen Drucktechniken, darunter auch Thermographie, Blindprägung, Folienkaschierung und Stahlstich. Damit lassen sich auf voluminösen Naturpapieren ungewöhnlich eindringliche Ergebnisse erzielen. Zu den Anwendungsbüchern gehören auch ausführliche technische Hinweise im Hinblick auf Litho, Druck und Weiterverarbeitung. Die Vorteile dieses Systems liegen auf der Hand:ein großer Fundus an Ideen ohne das Risiko des „Blindfluges" bei der Um-setzung in die Realität. Der wird zudem durch eine sachkundige Beratung vermieden. Seit 1958 schult Strathmore in Amerika die „Graphic Art Consultants" der Vertriebspartner - das sind Papiergroßhändler in 35 Ländern der Erde. Das mehrtägige Seminar unterrichtet die Agenturberater über die Rolle des Papieres im Grafikdesign, verschiedene Drucktechniken sowie neueste Trends in Sachen Papier und Design. Von den speziell eingesetzten Beratern erhalten Werbeagenturen oft die Anregungen und Informationen, die der Drucker mangels Zeit oder Kenntnissen nicht geben kann.

In der Angebotsbreite hat sich Strathmore auf den Bedarf der Werbeagenturen eingestellt. Von jeder Sorte wird ein Komplettprogramm angeboten, d.h. mehrere Gewichte im Papier -und Kartonbereich sowie Briefhüllen und passende Etiketten.

Strathmore hat eine europäische Zentrale in Bussum, Niederlande. Von dort erhalten die europäischen Großhändler eine speziell auf ihren Markt abgestimmte Verkaufsunterstützung. Das eigene

...gerhaus ermöglicht eine Belieferung innerhalb weniger Tage.

Die neueste Entwicklung

Umfangreiche Marktforschungen haben gezeigt, wie der Papierbedarf in der zweiten Hälfte der neunziger Jahre voraussichtlich aussehen wird.

Zentrale Forderung ist die Umweltverträglichkeit. Aus diesem Grund werden bei Strathmore nur noch Papiere produziert, die je nach Qualitätsanforderungen einen größtmöglichen Recyclinganteil besitzen. Auch der Einsatz von Baumwolle ist ökologisch sinnvoll, da es sich um einen vergleichsweise schnell nachwachsenden Rohstoff handelt. In der Papierproduktion werden zudem nur die zur Textilherstellung nicht geeigneten Randschichten der Baumwolle eingesetzt.

Ein weiterer Trend: Papier muß den Anforderungen an moderne Bürodrucker und neueste Schnelldruckmaschinen gerecht werden. Dazu brauchen sie eine relativ glatte und geschlossene Oberfläche, einen speziellen Feuchtegehalt und sollten auch im A 4 Format angeboten werden. Last but not least fordern die Werbetreibenden, daß auch ein hochwertiges Papier bezahlbar sein muß.

Das Ergebnis dieser Erkenntnisse hat bei Strathmore einen Namen: Elements. Eine umweltverträgliche Stoffzusammensetzung (50% Recyclinganteil) , die von der Fabrik garantierte Eignung für den Laserdrucker (bis 105 g/qm) und kostet ungefähr 10 % weniger als vergleichbare Sorten.

Das Papier entwickelte Produktmanager Bob Daigneault zusammen mit der New Yorker Werbeagentur Designframe. Sechs zarte Pastelltöne und die Grundelemente grafischer Gestaltung - lines, dots, squares, grid, grain und zickzack - geben Elements die neue ungewöhnliche Optik. Versuche zeigen, daß die im Papier eingebrachten Muster je nach Farbdichte und Deckfähigkeit der verwendeten Druckfarben sichtbar sind oder verschwinden. Ist das Muster gerade noch sichtbar, ergänzt es den Druck so, daß interessante Effekte im Druckbild entstehen können, ohne daß die farbige Struktur des Papieres dabei aufdringlich oder störend wirkt. Es kann sich eine ebenso interessante wie witzige Beziehung zwischen Papier und Druck entwickeln. Es gibt aber auch eine neutrale Version (solids).

Tim Sebastian von Designframe entwarf ein Musterbuch, das die sprachliche Verwendung der Gestaltungselemente in witzige Grafi-ken umsetzt (z.B. square-headed). Sebastian ist sehr angetan von der Zusammenarbeit mit Strathmore: „Mit einem Papierhersteller zusammenzuarbeiten, ermöglicht es Designern, die Kunst voranzutreiben." Bisher war diese Zusammenarbeit nur auf die Absatzförderung beschränkt. Die gemeinsame Erarbeitung von Elements von der Konzeption bis hin zur Po-sitionierung im Markt stellt ein echtes Novum dar. Daran hätte Horace Moses sicher seine Freude gehabt.

STRATHMORE -DIE PAPIERQUALITÄTEN

Americana hat eine sehr grobe, wellenartige Filznarbung. Je nach Betrachtungs-haltung wird eine andere Oberflächenstruktur sichtbar-

ein Papier mit multidimensionalen Effekten. Americana hat einen Recyclinganteil von 50%, ist in 11 kräftigen Farben und zwei Gewichten erhältlich; es wird vor allem als Umschlagqualität eingesetzt.

Grandee

ist die bekannteste filzgenarbte Sorte. Die strukturierte Oberfläche wird mit dem Egoutteur und im Anschluß an die Siebpartie mit Trockenfilzen erzielt. Grandee hat einen Altpapieranteil von 50% , ist in 13 Farben und zwei Gewichten erhältlich; durch die gute Farbwiedergabe und die hohe Opazität ist es ein geeigneter Druckträger für alle Arten von Druckobjekten.

Fiest

hat etwas wirklich Ungewöhnliches zu bieten, nämlich einen farbigen Büttenrand an den beiden langen Seiten. 9 Farbvarianten in zwei Gewichten machen dieses Papier zum idealen Trägermaterial für ausgefallene Einladungskarten, Glückwunschkarten oder Speisekarten.

Pastelle

hat eine authentische Filznarbung und einen Büttenrand an den beiden langen Seiten. Durch die elegante Farbpalette mit 12 feinabgestimmten Pastelltönen ist Pastelle das richtige Papier für alle Kommunikation im Bereich hochwertiger Markenartikel.

Rhododendron

ist die einzige geprägte Sorte im Programm. Das Muster, das handgewebtem irischem Leinen nachempfunden wurde, gibt diesem Papier mit 25% Baumwollanteil die elegant sportliche Note. Die Angebotsbreite von 2 Gewichten und 14 Farben macht es möglich, Rhododendron überall da einzusetzen, wo man die Verbindung von traditionellen Werten mit modernem Design demonstrieren möchte.

Renewal

hat eine maschinenglatte Oberfläche. Das Besondere an diesem umweltfreundlichen Papier mit 50% Recyclinganteil ist der Fasereinschluß. Zu den 7 Farben in der Version „dirty" gibt es auch noch die Variante „clean": das sind die gleichen Farben, aber ohne Fasereinschlüsse. Renewal dokumentiert auf ästhetisch ansprechende Weise Umweltbewußtsein.

Writing System

ist ein umfassendes Programm verschiedener Papiere für den Geschäftspostbereich. Man kann wählen zwischen 12 zarten Farbtönen, verschiedenen Oberflächen, und unterschiedlicher Stoffzusammensetzung. Dazu gibt es passende Etiketten und Briefhüllen. Ebenso hat man die Wahl zwischen Ausführungen mit und ohne Wasserzeichen. Dem Einsatzzweck entsprechend ist das Papier garantiert im Laserdrucker zu bedrucken und für Inkjet geeignet.

Elements

Elements ist farblich auf Strathmore Writing abgestimmt und in das Strathmore Writing System integriert.

Das Papier ist aufgrund seine technischen Eigenschaften universell einsetzbar, d.h. sowohl als Geschäftsausstattungspapier (Laserdruckgarantie) als auch als Auflagen- und Umschlagqualität.

STRATHMORE - PARCE QUE LE PAPIER C'EST PARTIE DE L'IMAGE DE MARQUE

L'ère du Far West était encore bien vivante dans les esprits lorsque Horace Moses fonda en 1892 la Mittineague Paper Company à West Springfield, Massachussetts. C'est peut-être pour cette raison qu'il a donné à sa fabrique de papier le nom d'une tribu indienne qui avait vécu dans la région.

La philosophie d'entreprise de Moses était aussi simple que convaincante. Il voulait produire des papiers de qualité supérieure, sortant de l'ordinaire, et proposer des services exceptionnels. Il était sans cesse à la recherche de nouvelles machines à papier qui lui permettent de fabriquer des types de papier peu communs. Il avait entendu dire qu'il existait en Angleterre une machine avec laquelle il était possible d'obtenir des bords frangeux ressemblant à s'y tromper à du papier à la cuve. Il se rendit donc en Europe, y trouva la machine qu'il cherchait et trouva par la même occasion un nom pour ses produits en Ecosse: Strathmore.

Le paysage pittoresque de la „Valley of Strathmore", où la bruyère et les chardons écossais étaient justement en fleurs, lui avait laissé un souvenir inoubliable. En 1898, il fit enregistrer le nom de „Strathmore" comme marque déposée et le chardon devint l'emblème de sa firme.

Horace Moses était persuadé que ses papiers auraient beaucoup de succès à la vente s'il parvenait à montrer leur beauté sous les formes les plus diverses. C'est ainsi qu'il est entré dans l'histoire du design américain en tant qu'éditeur du premier catalogue d'échantillons avec exemples d'applications. Il avait engagé spécialement dans ce but un imprimeur dans sa firme: Will Bradley allait se faire par la suite une réputation mondiale en tant que designer typographique et imprimeur de livres de haute valeur.

Les clients firent un accueil enthousiaste au catalogue d'échantillons ainsi qu'aux papiers et l'entreprise prit de l'extension. Une de ses nouvelles acquisitions, une fabrique d'enveloppes, allait lui permettre de proposer des enveloppes allant avec les différents types de papier, tout en restant fidèle à la légendaire qualité Strathmore.

Horace Moses décéda en 1947 à l'âge de 85 ans, et les gérants qui prirent sa succession n'étaient pas tous aussi géniaux que lui. En 1962, Strathmore fut vendu à Hammermill; depuis 1986, elle fait partie du plus grand groupe de fabrication de papier du monde: International Paper.

LA GAMME DE PRODUITS

Strathmore est de nos jours un des plus grands fournisseurs de papier dans trois domaines spécialisés:

Papiers à base de coton

C'est Strathmore qui détient aux USA la part la plus importante des types de papier renfermant 25 % de coton. Le mérite en revient avant tout au Strathmore Writing System. Ce système a été mis au point à la fin des années quatre-vingt et vient d'être entièrement remanié et adapté aux besoins du marché. Grâce aux perfectionnements techniques qui lui ont été apportés, il peut être utilisé sans problèmes sur toutes les imprimantes laser. A côté de différentes qualités de blanc, la gamme de coloris comporte également des „tons neutres de couleur" dan la fabrication desquels les pâtes de recyclage représentent u pourcentage élevé. Tout en étant de couleur, les papier fabriqués dans ces coloris sont néanmoins utilisables ave autant de souplesse qu'un papier blanc.

Papiers „Text & Cover"

Strathmore est connue avant tout pour ses qualités d'envelopp de couleur. Leurs marques de feutre authentiques sont l'emblèm de cette fabrique de papier. Les qualités Grandee, Americana Fiesta et Pastelle sont encore fabriquées de nos jours sur le machines à papier d'antan, qui ne travaillent guère plus vite qu'u artisan. Bien des fabriques ont déjà abandonné cette techniqu pour se tourner vers des processus de production beaucoup plu rapides. Strathmore au contraire s'efforce continuellement d concilier ces particularités avec les exigences du marché modern

Papier de dessin et peinture

Aux USA, Strathmore est le numéro un sur le marché des papiers d dessin et peinture. Ceux-ci vont des papiers 100 % coton aux pâte entièrement à base de bois. Ces papiers sont en vente exclusive au USA dans le commerce de détail spécialisé, par feuilles ou en blocs.

Un concept moderne de marketing

Strathmore s'adresse avant tout aux dessinateurs graphistes Car ceux-ci jouent un rôle décisif dans le choix du papier; d plus, ils sont toujours à la recherche de nouvelles qualités d papier et de nouveaux exemples d'applications. La tendance es non plus au simple catalogue d'échantillons, mais au catalogu combiné d'échantillons et d'applications. Des exemples de différentes techniques d'impression, entre autre thermographie, gaufrage à froid, contrecollage et gravure su acier, y sont présentés. Cela permet d'obtenir des résultats d plus bel effet sur les papiers non couchés volumineux. Le catalogues d'applications renferment également de renseignements techniques détaillés sur la lithographie l'impression et la transformation des papiers. Les avantages d ce système sont clairs: Il offre une mine d'idées qui peuvent êtr mises en oeuvre dans la pratique sans devoir se lancer l'aveuglette. Un service compétent d'information contribue pa ailleurs à éliminer les risques. Strathmore propose depuis 195 des stages de formation en Amérique aux „graphic ar consultants" de ses partenaires de distribution - des grossiste en papier de 35 pays du monde. Ce séminaire, qui dure plusieur jours, informe les consultants des agences de publicité sur l rôle du papier dans le design graphique, sur les différente techniques d'impression ainsi que sur les tendances nouvelle en matière de papier et de design. Et ce sont bien souvent le consultants qui fournissent aux agences de publicité les idées e les informations que l'imprimeur n'est pas en mesure de leu donner faute de temps ou de connaissances.

Strathmore a adapté son offre aux besoins des agences d publicité. La firme propose un programme complet pour chaqu type de papier, c.-à-d. plusieurs grammages de papier et de carto ainsi que les enveloppes et les étiquettes correspondantes.

Strathmore a un siège central en Europe, à Bussum, Pays-Bas. Celui-ci apporte aux grossistes européens un soutien spécialement adapté à leurs marchés respectifs. Son entrepôt lui permet d'effectuer des livraisons en quelques jours seulement.

La toute dernière évolution

Des études de marché détaillées ont montré quels seront vraisemblablement les besoins en papier durant la deuxième moitié des années 90. Une des exigences premières sera l'absence de pollution pour l'environnement. Pour cette raison, Strathmore ne fabrique plus que des papiers utilisant le pourcentage maximum de pâte de recyclage possible en fonction des exigences de qualité. L'utilisation du coton est également favorable sur le plan écologique car il s'agit d'une matière première renouvelable rapidement comparée aux autres matières. De plus, seules les couches marginales du coton, qui ne sont pas utilisées dans la fabrication textile, entrent dans la fabrication du papier.

Autre tendance: Le papier doit répondre aux exigences imparties aux imprimantes modernes de bureau et aux derniers modèles de machines à imprimer rapides. Il doit donc avoir une surface relativement lisse et fermée et doit également être proposé en format A4. Last but not least, les publicitaires attendent des papiers de qualité supérieure qu'ils soient néanmoins de prix abordable.

La somme de toutes ces exigences a un nom chez Strathmore: Elements. Ses caractéristiques: composition non polluante du papier (part des pâtes de recyclage 60 %), compatibilité garantie avec les imprimantes laser (jusqu'à 105 g/m2), coût approximatif: 10 % de moins que les types de papier comparables.

Ce papier a été mis au point par le chef de produit Bob Daigneault en collaboration avec l'agence de publicité new-yorkaise Designframe. Six tons pastel très doux et les éléments du design graphique - lines, dots, squares, grid, grain et zigzag - confèrent à Elements son aspect peu ordinaire. Des tests ont montré que les dessins dans le papier sont plus ou moins visibles, jusqu'à devenir invisibles, selon la densité spectrale et le pouvoir couvrant des encres d'imprimerie utilisées. Si le motif est à peine visible, il permet d'obtenir, combiné avec l'impression, des effets intéressants sans que la structure de couleur du papier soit trop voyante ou gênante. Il en résulte une interaction à la fois intéressante et amusante entre le papier et l'impression. Mais il existe également une version neutre (solids).

Jim Sebastian de l'agence Designframe a créé un catalogue d'échantillons où les éléments d'un nom sont remplacés par des symboles graphiques combinés de manière amusante (p. ex. square-headed). Sebastian est très satisfait de la collaboration avec Strathmore: „Travailler avec un fabricant de papier permet aux designers de faire progresser l'art." Jusqu'ici, cette collaboration était limitée à la promotion des ventes. L'élaboration en commun d'Elements, de la conception au positionnement sur le marché, est une nouveauté sans précédent. Et cela aurait certainement fait très plaisir à Horace Moses.

Les papiers Strathmore sont en vente chez (revendeur du pays concerné). Il faut s'attendre à des délais de livraison longs pour les types de papier non disponibles de stock.

STRATHMORE - LES QUALITÉS DE PAPIER

Americana

porte une marque de feutre ondulée très accentuée. Sa structure de surface varie selon l'angle du regard - un papier aux effets multidimensionnels. Americana comporte 50 % de matière recyclée ; il est disponible en 11 coloris soutenus et deux poids - il est tout particulièrement employé pour les couvertures.

Grandee

est le plus renommé parmi les papiers marqués au feutre. Sa surface structurée est obtenue par le passage sur l'égoutteur puis sur la table de fabrication à feutres sécheurs. Grandee est composé à 50 % de vieux papiers recyclés : il est disponible en 13 coloris et deux poids - grâce à une bonne reproduction des couleurs et à une opacité élevée, il forme un excellent support d'impression.

Fiesta

est un papier peu ordinaire qui se distingue par des bords frangeux colorés qui longent la feuille.
9 coloris et deux poids font de ce papier un support idéal pour des cartes d'invitation, des cartes de vœux ou des menus originaux.

Pastelle

présente une marque de feutre authentique ainsi que des bords frangeux le long de la feuille.
Avec sa gamme de coloris élégants comportant 12 nuances pastel harmonieuses, Pastelle est parfaitement adapté à tout ce qui touche à la communication dans le secteur des articles de marque.

Rhododendron

est le seul papier gaufré de la gamme. Son motif inspiré du lin irlandais tissé à la main procure une touche d'élégance sportive à ce papier qui contient 25 % de coton.
2 poids et 14 coloris permettent d'utiliser Rhododendron à chaque fois que l'on souhaite combiner les valeurs traditionnelles et le design moderne.

Renewal

possède une surface satinée sur calandre. Respectueux de l'environnement avec 50 % de matière recyclée, ce papier se distingue par des insertions de fibres. Il est disponible en 7 coloris, avec insertions pour la version „dirty" et sans insertions pour la version „clean."
Renewal est l'expression réussie d'une alliance entre l'esthétique et le respect de l'environnement.

Writing System

est une gamme complète de différents papiers destinés à la correspondance commerciale. On a le choix entre 12 couleurs tendres, différentes surfaces et combinaisons de chiffons. Viennent s'y ajouter étiquettes et enveloppes assorties. Il y a également possibilité d'opter ou non pour une marque filigranée. Comme l'exige son domaine d'utilisation, il est adapté aux imprimantes laser ou à jet d'encre.

Elements

Les coloris de Elements s'harmonisent avec Strathmore Writing et s'intègrent au

Strathmore Writing System.

Grâce à ses qualités techniques, ce papier est utilisable dans tous les domaines, c'est-à-dire aussi bien au bureau (impression laser garantie), que pour l'édition de brochures ou la fabrication de couvertures.

BECKETT PAPERS - INNOVATION IS THE KEY TO SUCCESS

Founded in 1848 by William Beckett, the son of an early Ohio settler, Beckett is the fourth oldest operating fine paper mill in the United States; a true industry pioneer.

In the years to follow, Beckett Papers take credit for an unequaled list of industry innovations. The first premium lithographic paper, the first fluorescent lithographic paper, first use of corrugated cartons, first use of polyethylene-lined cartons, and first use of polyethylene wrap on skids are among such innovations.

Beckett's innovation did not stop with the acquisition of the mill by Hammermill Paper in 1959. First came the introduction of the industry of lightweight duplex papers. Next, in 1970, Beckett took advantage of its expertise in embossing and introduced a comprehensive line of linen printing and writing papers called Cambric. Beckett continued its innovations in embossing during the 1980's with introductions of the grade lines Ridge and Enhance!.

In 1986 the Hammermill Paper Group was acquired by the world's largest paper producer: International Paper. The vast resources of International Paper allowed Beckett to continue its rich tradition of innovations. In 1991, Beckett Papers was the first fine paper mill to manufacture its complete product line with recycled fiber.

Nowadays, Beckett Papers maintains a modern plant with three paper machines, rewinding and laminating capabilities, and a large finishing department. The mill can produce more than 250,000 different products, in an assortment of weights, finishes, and colors.

Beckett papers are sold by independent wholesale paper merchants in every major city in North America as well as in many European countries. All merchants have the exclusive sales rights for their country.

PRODUCT LINES

Beckett's environmental awareness is evident in most of its contemporary line-up of six premium grades, each of which includes recycled fibre content. The mill combines at least 50% recycled content (10% post consumer) with the highest standards of product quality.

Beckett grades:

- Cambric: with a premium linen finish
- R.S.V.P.: a true felt finish for prestigious look and feel
- Ridge: deeply grooved finish that adds a look of distinction
- Enhance!: with a satiny finish and contemporary colour palette
- Concept: versatile with three finishes and environmental appeal
- Beckett Expression: an affordable premium paper with 24% post consumer waste content and a smooth finish that invites ink coverage.

MARKETING ACTIVITIES

- The mill operates the Beckett Idea Center as a resource for complete projects accomplished with Beckett Papers. "Great ideas demand great papers" the Beckett motto attests. With its courteous service, paper samples, and promotions, the center is a valuable creative resource that demonstrates the printability of Beckett papers.

- Merchant Specification Conference: Specification representatives from the States and Europe are provided with information on the role of paper in graphic design. They also receive useful hints on how Beckett papers can be promoted successfully. The conference is held once a year and lasts for three days.

- Promotional Items: Beckett Papers prints samples, both in-house designs and commercial, to give designers inspiration for creative paper use. These samples are welcome in ad agencies and are handed out and explained by the graphic art consultants of the paper merchants.

- Beckett honors award: This is a competition held twice a year, in June and December. Judging for each contest takes place in different host cities and is conducted by a panel of designers, printers, and merchant art consultants. The contest declares three winners in two categories–business communication and general. All winning entries receive Beckett Honors Tiffany crystal stars to commemorate the event, while individual crystal stars are awarded to the designer, printer, and end user of each piece. Entries from all over the world are judged.

THE BECKETT GRADES

Enhance!

A pretty name for a pretty paper. No question. Merely the embossing turns each sheet into a material of which dreams are made. Light and bright, warm and comforting, capricious lovers of beautiful paper choose Enhance! in any one of the five mediterranean marble shades.

R.S.V.P.

Close your eyes and enjoy this paper as a sensorial treat. It's extraordinarily thick, but maintains a smoothness which runs like cream through your fingers. And the look: very distinctive, very honest, with fine color nuances. It's not hard to appreciate the tranquil silence of this tactile experience.

Ridge

Ridged–that is exactly what the paper's embossing looks like. Ridged with clear, linear parallels, giving the paper a cool and technical elegance. A thrilling contrast is the smooth surface of the paper which takes away all severity from the linear pattern. Another surprise is the smooth back. Ridge has more than just one good side.

Expression

Startling at first glance, these natural clear colors suggest a sunny winter afternoon cast into paper. The first touch is almost a shock– incredibly soft, incredibly smooth. What a material to design on. It's hard to believe that it contains 50% recovered fibers. Without hesitation, the hand reaches out once more, for another impression of Expression.

Cambric

A paper like Irish linen: strong, fine, and high-quality. The wide variety of colors and embossing make it possible for Cambric to always appear new and different. As a letterhead paper–in discreet colors and simple design–it gives the impression of success. With loud colors and interesting fibers it provides the perfect background for a private letter that looks altogether different.

ECKETT PAPERS - INNOVATION HEISST DER SCHLÜSSEL ZUM ERFOLG

eckett wurde 1848 von William Beckett, dem Sohn eines frühen edlers in Ohio, gegründet und ist damit als Pionier der Branche e viertälteste Feinpapierfabrik in den Vereinigten Staaten.

eit das Unternehmen besteht, kann Beckett Papers eine vergleichliche Reihe von Innovationen in der Papierbranche erweisen. Zu diesen Innovationen gehören das erste hochwertige thografiepapier, das erste fluoreszierende Lithografiepapier, der ste Einsatz von Wellpappe, von mit PE-Film ausgekleideten artons und von PE-folienverschweißten Ladegestellen.

ammermill Paper erwarb die Fabrik 1959 und setzte diese twicklung fort. Zuerst wurden leichte Duplexpapiere eingeführt. 970 konnte Beckett auf ihre Erfahrung im Prägen zurückgreifen nd führte ein umfangreiches Programm von leinengeprägten ruck- und Schreibpapieren ein - Cambric. Diese Prägeinnovationen urden in den achtziger Jahren mit der Einführung der ualitätssorten Ridge und Enhance! fortgeführt.

986 wurde der Hammermill Paper Konzern von International Paper, em weltweit größten Papierhersteller, erworben. Dank der hohen essourcen von International Paper konnte Beckett das bereits ekannte Innovationsstreben weiterführen: Im Jahre 1991 war eckett der erste Feinpapierhersteller, der seine Produktpalette aus iederverwerteten Fasern herstellte.

eute unterhält Beckett Papers eine moderne Fabrik mit drei apiermaschinen, Umroll- und Kaschiereinrichtungen sowie eine roße Veredelungsabteilung. Die Fabrik kann über 250.000 erschiedene Produkte in verschiedenen Gewichten, Oberflächen und arben herstellen.

eckett Papiere werden über unabhängige Papiergroßhändler in eder wichtigen Stadt in Nordamerika sowie in vielen europäischen ändern vertrieben. Alle Händler haben für ihr Land das leinverkaufsrecht.

RODUKTLINIEN

as Umweltbewußtsein von Beckett ist bei den meisten apierqualitäten der heutigen Produktpalette sichtbar, die llesamt einen Anteil wiederverwendeter Fasern haben. Mindestens 50 Prozent Recyclingfasern (10% post consumer) werden in der Papierfabrik mit dem höchsten Qualitätsmaßstab ombiniert.

ie Qualitäten von Beckett:
- Cambric: mit hochwertiger Leinenstruktur
- R.S.V.P.: eine Filzoberfläche, Genuß für Augen und Hände
- Ridge: edle Ausstrahlung dank gerillter Oberfläche
- Enhance!: mit einer Satinstruktur und moderner Farbauswahl
- Concept: vielseitig mit drei Oberflächenstrukturen mit Umwelt- harakter
- Beckett Expression: günstiges Qualitätspapier mit 24 Prozent ltpapieranteil und einer glatten Oberfläche, die Tinte gut aufnimmt

Marketingaktivitäten

- Die Papierfabrik unterhält das Beckett Idea Center als Fundus für mit Beckett Papieren gedruckte Muster. Das Motto von Beckett erspricht „Gutes Papier für gute Ideen". Das Center bietet mit dem reundlichen Service, Papiermustern und Verkaufsförderungs- maßnahmen kreative Ideen, die die Bedruckbarkeit der apiersorten von Beckett unter Beweis stellen.
- Händlerkonferenz: Die Vertreter aus den Vereinigten Staaten und Europa erhalten auf dieser Konferenz sehr viele Informationen über die Rolle des Papiers in der Grafikbranche sowie nützliche Tips, wie das Papier von Beckett erfolgreich vermarktet werden kann. Die dreitätige Konferenz findet einmal pro Jahr statt.
- Druckmuster: Beckett Papers druckt viele Proben, die selbst oder extern gestaltet werden, um den Designern Inspirationen zur kreativen Nutzung von Papier zu geben. Diese kostenlosen Proben werden gerne von Werbeagenturen angenommen und von den Grafikberatern der Papierhändler erklärt.
- Beckett honors award: Dieser Wettbewerb findet in verschiedenen Städten zweimal jährlich im Juni bzw. Dezember statt. Die Preisrichter sind Designer, Drucker und Grafikberater der Händler. In den beiden Kategorien „Werbung" und „Allgemeines" werden jeweils drei Gewinner benannt. Alle Gewinner erhalten die „Tiffany-Kristallsterne" als Erinnerung an dieses Ereignis. Dem Designer, Drucker und Endverbraucher jedes prämierten Stückes werden einzelne Sterne verliehen. Teilnehmer aus der ganzen Welt sind zum Wettbewerb eingeladen.

BECKETT - DIE PAPIERQUALITÄTEN

Expression

13 klare natürliche Farben in zwei Gewichten und die ungewöhnlich zarte, samtige Oberfläche zeichnen diese Qualität aus. Expression besteht zu 50 % aus wiederverwendeten Rohstoffen und eignet sich sehr gut für alle Druckverfahren. Das Angebot wird ergänzt durch passende Briefhüllen, Expression ist damit bestens für einen vielseitigen Einsatz gerüstet. R.S.V.P. Die authentische Filzmarkierung verleiht diesem Papier sein unverwechselbares Aussehen und die voluminöse Haptik.

R.S.V.P.

eignet sich als Auflagenpapier, aber auch sehr gut als Umschlag-qualität, es ist bis 270 g/qm erhältlich. Die Wahl zwischen den13 fein nuancierten Farben fällt schwer; das fertige Druckergebnis wird jeden Empfänger begeistern, der auf Natürlichkeit und Individualität Wert legt.

Ridge

Furche - das ist die deutsche Entsprechung für Ridge. So sieht die Prägung des Papieres aus, es ist von klaren linearen Parallelen durchfurcht. In Kombination mit der samtigen Oberfläche ist das ein reizvoller Kontrast und gibt dem Papier eine kühle Eleganz. 8 Farben und zwei Gewichte bieten die ideale Grundlage für viele Gestaltungsmöglichleiten.

Enhance

Enhance - Verschönerung, ein guter Name für ein schönes Papier. Die zarte stoffähnliche Oberflächenprägung kommt in außergewöhnlich hellen oder warmen Farbtönen daher. Einige davon tragen eine mediterran anmutende Marmorschattierung.

Cambric

Ein Papier, das die Anmutung von irischem Leinen hat. Eine breite Farbpalette ermöglicht einen vielfätigen Einsatz. Als gediegenes Geschäftspapier hat Cambric einen ebenso perfekten Auftritt wie als freche Privatpost in knallbunten Farben oder mit melierten Fasern.

Sämtliche Qualitäten sind über den Feinpapiergroßhandel zu beziehen. Dort gibt es auch Muster für Layouts oder Andrucke.

BECKETT PAPERS - INNOVATION EST LA CLÉ DU SUCCÈS

La société fut fondée en 1848 par William Beckett, fils d'un colon très tôt établi dans l'Ohio. Beckett est la quatrième parmi les plus anciennes manufactures de papier surfin encore en opération aux Etats-Unis. Elle fait figure de véritable pionnier du secteur industriel. Au cours des années qui suivent sa fondation, Beckett Papers produit une quantité inégalable d'innovations dont voici quelques exemples : le premier papier de qualité supérieure pour impression lithographique, le premier papier fluorescent pour impression lithographique, la première utilisation du carton ondulé, la première utilisation de carton garni de polyéthylène et la première utilisation d'une feuille de polyéthylène pour la protection des casiers de stockage.

Rachetée par Hammermill Paper en 1959, Beckett ne cesse pas pour autant de lancer des nouveautés sur le marché. Citons, en premier lieu, l'introduction des papiers duplex légers. Puis, en 1970, avantagée par l'avance qu'elle possède dans le domaine du gaufrage, la société Beckett est la première à proposer une gamme diversifiée de papier toilé et de papier à lettres qui reçoit le nom de Cambric. Beckett continue d'innover dans le domaine du gaufrage au cours des années 80 en lançant les séries de qualité supérieure Ridge et Enhance.

En 1986, le Hammermill Paper Group est racheté par le plus grand fabricant de papier du monde : International Paper. Les vastes ressources de International Paper permettent à Beckett de rester fidèle à sa tradition innovatrice. En 1991, Beckett Papers est le premier à utiliser des fibres recyclées pour toute sa ligne de produits. Aujourd'hui, Beckett Papers possède une usine moderne abritant trois machines à papier, des équipements d'enroulage et de contrecollage ainsi qu'un grand atelier de finissage. La manufacture produit plus de 250 000 produits différents, dans un assortiment de poids, d'apprêts et de couleurs.

Les papiers fabriqués par Beckett sont vendus par des grossistes indépendants dans toutes les grandes villes d'Amérique du Nord ainsi que dans de nombreux pays européens. Tous ces négociants détiennent des droits de vente exclusifs dans leur pays respectif.

Lignes de produits

Beckett est une société soucieuse de préserver l'environnement, ce qui se traduit dans la plupart de ses six lignes de produits de qualité supérieure qui contiennent toutes des fibres recyclées. La manufacture allie une teneur minimum de 50 % de produits recyclés (10 % post consommateur) aux exigences de qualité les plus sévères.

Les qualités Beckett :

Cambric : un apprêt toilé de première qualité

R.S.V.P. : un apprêt feutré authentique pour un aspect et un toucher prestigieux

Ridge : structure à rainures profondes qui ajoute une note distinguée

Enhance: un apprêt satiné et une palette de couleurs contemporaines

Concept: polyvalent avec trois finitions et un souci réel de l'environnement

Beckett Expression : un papier de qualité supérieur contenant 24 % de déchets post consommateur, dont l'apprêt velouté invite à l'écriture, proposé à un prix abordable

Activités de marketing

La manufacture gère le Beckett Idea Center qui regroupe les projets réalisés sur les papiers Beckett. Le slogan le dit bien „Les grandes idées méritent un grand papier". Avec un service courtois, des échantillons de papier et des campagnes promotionnelles, ce centre est une source de créativité très précieuse qui démontre les qualités des impressions obtenues avec les papiers Beckett.

• Merchant Specification Conference : les agents responsables des caractéristiques techniques pour les Etats-Unis et l'Europe apprennent une foule de choses concernant le rôle du papier dans la conception graphique. Ils obtiennent également une multitude de renseignements utiles à une promotion réussie des papiers Beckett. La conférence se tient une fois par an et dure trois jours.

• Articles promotionnels : Beckett Papers imprime une multitude d'échantillons, de conception interne ou externe, pour aider les designers dans leurs recherches d'idées nouvelles appliquées au papier. Ces échantillons sont très bien accueillis par les agences de publicité. Ils sont distribués (gratuitement) et commentés par les conseillers artistiques des grossistes.

• Beckett honors award : il s'agit d'un concours qui a lieu deux fois par an, en juin et en décembre. Les compétitions se déroulent dans différentes villes sous l'autorité d'un jury composé de designers, d'imprimeurs et des conseillers artistiques des négociants. Trois lauréats sont désignés dans deux catégories - communication commerciale et domaine général. Tous les produits retenus reçoivent la récompense du Beckett Honors : les étoiles de cristal Tiffany pour commémorer l'événement. Des étoiles de cristal individuelles sont remises aux designers, imprimeurs et utilisateurs de chaque article. Les produits du monde entier sont admis à participer au concours.

BECKETT - LES QUALITÉS DE PAPIER

Expression

13 coloris naturels disponibles en deux poids et une surface particulièrement douce et veloutée caractérisent cette qualité de papier. Expression est composé à 50 % de matières premières recyclées et se prête fort bien à tous les processus d'impression. L'offre est enrichie d'enveloppes assorties. Expression est donc parfaitement adapté à une utilisation diversifiée.

R.S.V.P.

L'authenticité de sa marque de feutre donne à ce papier son aspect inimitable et une agréable sensation d'épaisseur au toucher. R.S.V.P. peut être employé comme papier d'édition mais également sans problème pour couvrir les brochures. Son poids peut aller jusqu'à 270 g/m2. Le choix entre 13 coloris aux nuances subtiles est difficile ; tous ceux qui attachent de l'importance à l'aspect naturel et à l'individualité seront enthousiasmés par sa qualité d'impression.

Ridge

Nervure - tel est l'équivalent français de Ridge. C'est d'ailleurs ainsi que se présente ce papier parcouru de nervures longitudinales parallèles. Combinées au velouté de la surface, elles produisent un contraste séduisant qui donne au papier sa sobre élégance. 8 coloris et deux poids sont un point de départ idéal à la créativité.

Enhance

Enhance - embellissement, quel nom magnifique pour un beau papier. La fine structure de surface qui évoque une étoffe affiche des tons clairs ou chauds. Certains d'entre eux présentent une marbrure aux réminiscences méditerranéennes.

Cambric

Un papier aux allures de lin irlandais. Sa large palette de coloris permet un emploi diversifié. Sous sa version classique destinée à la correspondance commerciale, Cambric produit tout autant d'effet que dans les couleurs éclatantes ou avec les fibres chinées réservées à une correspondance privée plus désinvolte.

Austria: IT Papier,
Belgium: PB Papier NV,
Cyprus: George
C. Kazinos & Co.,
Denmark: Albatross Papir,
France: Aussedat Rey
Distribution,
Germany: Schneidersöhne
Papier,
Israel: Prelude Ltd,
Italy: Perego Carta,
Malta: Beck Graphis Ltd,
Norway: Carl Emil AS,
Portugal: Spectra,
Spain: Royal Paper & Co.,
Switzerland: Mühleback AG
Graphic,
Sweden: Svenskt Papper AB,
The Netherlands:
Lutkie & Smit Papier and
Scaldia Papier, Turkey:
Unirep Trading & Agency Inc.,
United Kingdom: G.F.
Smith & Son Ltd.
Kenya: Proost Paper Ltd. ,
South Africa: Spicers

CARIBBEAN, CENTRAL-AND
SOUTH AMERICA
Sales Office in Memphis,
TN 38197 USA
Julio Cepeda,
phone: (+1) 901 763 7613
fax: (+1) 901 763 7169
Strathmore is represented in
the following countries:
Argentina: Dimagraf SACI,
Bolivia: GMS Bolivia,
Brazil: VIP Papers,
Chile: GMS Productos Graficos,

Colombia: Bico Inter-national,
Guatemala: Codelsa,
Jamaica: H.G.M. Walker Ltd.,
Mexico: Importaciones
y Distribuciones
Lumen SA de CV.,
Peru: GMS Distribuidora
Grafica S.A.,
Puerto Rico: American
Paper Corporation,
Uruguay: José Castiglioni S.A.,
Venezuela: Casa Hellmund
& CIA S.A.

ASIA AND THE PACIFIC:
Sales Office in Hong Kong
Albert C. Lau,
phone: (+852) 2586 8818
fax: (+852) 2824 3035
Strathmore is represented in
the following countries:
China: Hiap Moh Paper,
Indonesia: PT Armada
Pratama and PT Surya
Palacejaya,
Japan: JMC Corporation,
Malaysia: Hiap Moh
Paper Co. (m) Sdn. Bhd.,
Philippines: Star Paper
Corporation,
Singapore: Hiap Moh
Corporation,
Taiwan R.O.C.: Circle Trading
Company Ltd.,
Thailand: D.H.A. Siamwalle Ltd.
Australia: Alexander
Moir & Co. Pty. Ltd., K.W.
Dogelt Pty. Ltd.,
Bommerang Paper,
New Zealand: B.J. Ball Papers

BECKETT PAPERS
Two Gateway Boulevard
East Granby, CT 06026 USA
phone: (+1) 800 543 1188
fax: (+1) 800 392 9192

Beckett Papers is part of
INTERNATIONAL PAPER'S
Fine Papers Division
To recieve more information
about Beckett Papers
and your home merchant,
please contact one of the
following offices:

UNITED STATES:
Beckett Papers is
represented in every state of
the union. For full information
please contact
(+1) 800 423 2259
or the Fine Paper Head Office
East Granby, CT 06026
Jeannie Means,
phone: (+1) 860 844 2413
fax: (+1) 860 844 2552

EUROPE, MIDDLE EAST,
AND AFRICA
Strathmore Beckett
International
Oude Apeldoornseweg 26
7333 NS Apeldoom,
The Netherlands
Gitte Demmers
phone (+31) 55 5384553
fax (+31) 55 5384550
Beckett is represented
in the following countries:
Austria: Europapier and

Eu-RO Handelsgellschaft
m.b.H., Belgium: Epacar,
Cyprus: George
G. Kazinos & Co.,
Denmark: Albatross Papir,
France: Muller Renage,
Germany: Römerturm,
Israel: Prelude Ltd,
Italy: Perego Carta,
Norway: Carl Emil AS,
Portugal: Spectra,
Spain: Papelera
del Gaya, Switzerland:
Mühlebach AG Graphic,
Sweden: Svenskt Papper AB,
The Netherlands:
Bührmann-Ubbens Papier,
United Kingdom:
G.F. Smith & Son, Ltd.,
Kenya: Proost Paper
(E.A.) Ltd.
South Africa: Spicers

CARIBBEAN, CENTRAL- AND
SOUTH AMERICA
Sales Office
in Memphis, TN, 38197, USA
Julio Cepeda,
phone: (+1) 901 763 7613
fax: (+1) 901 763 7169
Beckett is represented in
the following countries:
Argentina: Dimagraf SACI,
Bolivia: GMS Bolivia,
Brazil: VIP Papers, Chile:
GMS Productos Graficos,
Colombia: Propal SA,
Guatemala: Codelsa,
Honduras: AM Capens &
Sons Inc., Jamaica: H.G.M.

Walker Ltd., Mexico:
Importaciones y
Distribuciones
Lumen SA de CV.,
Peru: GMS Distribuidora
Grafica S.A., Puerto Rico:
American Paper
Corporation,
Uruguay: José Castiglioni S.A.,
Venezuela:
Dasa Hellmund +CIA S.A.

ASIA AND THE PACIFIC:
Sales office in Hong Kong
Albert C. Lau,
phone: (+852) 2586 8818,
fax: (+852) 2824 3035
Beckett is represented in
the following countries:
China: Hiap Moh Paper,
Indonesia: PT Armada
Pratama and PT Surya
Palacejaya,
Japan: JMC Corporation,
Korea: Kye Sung
Corporation and Yousun
Corporation,
Malaysia: Hiap Moh Paper
Co. (M) Sdn. Bhd.,
Phillipines: Star Paper
Corporation, Singapore: Hiap
Moh Corporation,
Taiwan R.O.C.: Circle
Trading Company Ltd.,
Thailand: D.H.A. Siamwalle
Ltd. Australia: Alexander
Moir & Co. Pty. Ltd., K.W.
Dogelt Pty. Ltd., Boomerang
Paper, New Zealand:
B.J. Ball Papers

This section is printed on Strathmore Renewal, Chamois, 118 grs (text 80)